Economic
Development
Marketing
2nd Edition

Rau,

Enjoy the book!

Also by Anatalio Ubalde and Eric Simundza

Economic Development Online
Anatalio C. Ubalde and Andrew Krueger
2011

Economic Development Marketing: Present and Future
Anatalio C. Ubalde and Eric Simundza
2008

Economic Development Marketing

2nd Edition

Anatalio C. Ubalde
& Eric Simundza

For more information, visit:

GIS Planning:
www.GISplanning.com

ZoomProspector:
www.ZoomProspector.com

SizeUp:
www.SizeUp.com

ISBN: 978-0-692-01877-4

Printed in the United States of America

10 9 8 7 6 5 4 3 2 1

Contents

12. Case Studies (continued)

Introduction

"You need the kind of objectivity that makes you forget everything you've heard, clear the table, and do a factual study like a scientist would."

- Steve Wozniak, Co-Founder, Apple

The challenging state of the economy since 2008 has forced economic development agencies across the country to reevaluate every tool in their traditional tool box, and to think creatively about how to move forward in a new economic and operational reality. The maxim goes, "If it ain't broke, don't fix it," and good economic times can make even broken efforts look good. Perhaps the follow up to that saying should be "if you don't know it's broke, it's really hard to fix it." These types of blind spots can incapacitate an organization. This book will open your eyes to what is broken, what needs fixing, and what's working in economic development marketing.

There are many ways that communities have been marketed. Some of the marketing tactics that have historically worked continue to work, but many are not effective anymore and are facing extinction under new economic and communication paradigms.

Few people in the economic development profession graduate with a college degree in economic development. Instead, much of the professional education comes on-the-job and by attending conferences or professional development trainings. A problem with the economic development marketing training courses is that many of the introductory classes should be titled "A History of Economic Development Marketing" but they are called "An Introduction to Economic Development Marketing." So the people attending the classes are confused because they think they are getting an introduction when they are actually getting a history. And it's a history of many economic development marketing strategies that worked in the past but don't work well anymore. Unfortunately, some of those attending leave thinking that all marketing strategies are equal when they really aren't.

Economic development marketing is evolving. I saw these changes in communication, technology, and new media unfolding when I worked in local economic development. The transformation became clearer to me as I moved to the private sector to start GIS Planning and worked across North America serving hundreds of communities, from the largest cities, states, and utility companies to the many small and medium sized communities.

One of my frustrations related to talking about the changes in marketing places was that there was limited data with which to measure these changes. Sometimes at national conferences when experts within our profession would quote percentages and statistics, I would ask them for their information sources and they would tell me "Oh, I think it's about that much." Unfortunately for the people that heard their speeches and were going to take action based on them, they thought those numbers were objectively quantified.

There was very little existing national research that was trustworthy or reliable. One of the few exceptions to this was the enlightening research by Development Counsellors International (DCI) that surveyed businesses and site selectors. However, what we were interested in was an understanding of the behavior and programs "on the ground" in economic development organizations (EDOs) across the USA that practice marketing.

So I developed a partnership with the University of California at Berkeley to design and implement a national survey about economic development marketing, and then to analyze the results. Like the research of this book, two surveys were created. The first was given to economic development practitioners. The second was given to corporate real estate professionals and site selection consultants responsible for making or influencing corporate site location decisions.

When we published the first book, the results had a significant impact on the economic development profession because the results illuminated practices economic development professionals (ED pros) needed to change. The survey revealed, among other things, that ED pros were significantly investing in marketing that didn't work well; the Internet surpassed face-to-face marketing in effectiveness; and the most effective marketing was often found in unexpected types of EDOs.

Thousands of ED pros and policy makers have read and own the first edition of this book. The desire for the book's information exceeded our expectations, and the way that ED pros have embraced the findings in their work is encouraging. Although, as this book will show, change is slow. Be that as it may, I often hear people talking about the findings of the book and I'm pleased that the content of our first book has affected the thinking and policy decisions of so many ED pros.

An important reason to do research is that you want to be surprised, and we were definitely surprised by the responses of this latest study. The results are contained in this book, and I won't summarize them in this introduction except to say our profession is improving in some areas and has plenty of room to improve in others, as can be seen from the time-series data that is published here for the first time. Making changes toward more effective strategies will give organizations a meaningful competitive advantage.

Another reason we pursued this survey is because GIS Planning needs to deeply understand the changes happening in the economic development profession so we can continue to stay ahead of the trends, anticipate changes, and develop new ways to make our clients the most successful in effective economic development.

Perhaps the most important reason for this survey is that as ED pros we need to get better. Many, if not most, of the EDOs in the USA are publicly funded through taxes on the businesses and residents of the community. We must be good stewards of these public resources and not waste people's money on marketing that doesn't produce results. Also, the work we do is important. We may not save lives like an emergency room doctor, but we have the opportunity to improve lives.

I learned very early on while working in local economic development that it was an amazing feeling when someone came up to me to thank me for helping a business open in my city because it gave them a better job. And to the readers of this book, since I imagine it's mostly ED pros reading this, my story is your story and the story of every economic developer who has been thanked by someone who got a new job, a better job, or a path to better employment because of the work you do in your office. Jobs enable so many things in people's lives, ranging from paying the mortgage to creating the self-esteem that results from having a job. Although businesses create jobs, ED pros can help foster their success.

So read this book and then let's get to work. We have people to help, so let's not waste any time, money, or marketing.

Anatalio C. Ubalde
San Francisco, California

Summary

There are many things that can be said of the start of the 2010s. "Business as usual" is certainly not one of them. The Great Recession has changed a vast number of lives along with some of our most basic underlying assumptions about the structure of the global economy. The far-reaching impacts of the economic crisis on major industries and established companies have prompted communities to increase their focus on damage control and holding on to what they have, in addition to trying to attract businesses from the outside. Mindful that startup activity historically increases in recessionary times, many progressive economic development groups have worked to promote entrepreneurship and encourage the growth of small businesses.

On the technology front, social media has evolved from a time-consuming diversion for teens to an essential tool for marketers. The rapid growth of companies like Facebook and LinkedIn, both of which became public in the beginning of the new decade, pointed to social media and the larger tech sector as a rare bright spot in an otherwise bleak national economic climate.

In the summer of 2008, when the economy was strong, we released *Economic Development Marketing: Present and Future*. The book used the results of surveys of both ED pros and corporate site selectors to shine a light on how communities promoted themselves, looking at all angles from the financial to the psychological to the technical. Enough has changed since then that we decided it was high time to ask the same audiences how the past few years have impacted their work, and their answers resulted in several key findings:

- EDOs feel more positively about the effectiveness of most of the marketing strategies in their toolbox than ever before, and dramatically more than when asked during the depths of the recession. EDOs also feel better about the efficacy of their marketing programs in general than in years past.
- The most effective marketing strategy for economic development is the organization's website, agreed upon by both ED pros and site selectors. Face-to-face marketing strategies, which were already given high marks in our last survey, went up the rankings, as the second and third most effective marketing strategies require personal contact.
- EDOs' budget allocations for marketing strategies do not always correlate with the effectiveness of each strategy. This indicates a lag between awareness and action, made even more glaring given that most of these same discrepancies were revealed in the first edition. However, highly effective strategies that involve personal contact have taken budget share away from ineffective strategies that involve printed materials.
- The website was reported by site selectors to be the first point of contact with an EDO during the site selection decision making process, rather than personal interaction with staff. 97% of site selectors visit websites of EDOs during the process of site selection.
- EDOs are making more elements of their websites interactive, and they are making greater use of website analytics.
- Effective marketers update their websites with greater frequency and more often include GIS tools for site selection analysis.
- EDOs utilize a variety of social media platforms, though ED pros tend to be less active on LinkedIn than site selectors, which poses an opportunity for EDOs that want to more effectively reach their audience.
- Online advertising is growing among EDOs in both its use and its perception of effectiveness.
- EDOs serving larger areas that have more resources at their disposal give marketing a larger budget share than smaller EDOs.

- The majority of EDOs are marketing to a national or global audience of businesses.
- Lead generation is the top measure of marketing success for EDOs, and the amount of jobs created is the top measure of success for organizations overall.
- The industries most targeted by EDOs differ from those that are served by corporate real estate professionals and site selectors, however they are quite aligned in their targeting of traditional manufacturing. ED pros place more emphasis on the new subsectors of manufacturing, while site selectors place greater emphasis than EDOs on locating corporate headquarters.

This book begins with a brief look at the general priorities of EDOs and where marketing fits within that scheme. It then demonstrates which marketing strategies are most and least effective, followed by a discussion of how EDOs allocate their budgets among these strategies and for marketing as a whole.

We next examine the geographic coverage of marketing as well as the industries targeted. After a brief look at the prevalence of directories for locations as well as EDOs, the discussion shifts to the sources of information utilized by corporate real estate professionals during the site selection process. The focus then analyzes economic development websites, including which resources EDOs typically provide on their websites and how they are maintained.

Following the section on websites is a chapter dedicated to social media and its utility within economic development, something new to this edition. The book wraps up its discussion of marketing strategies with a look at how EDOs benchmark the success of the entire organization and of marketing in particular. To illustrate some of the best practices discussed elsewhere in the book, we close with a selection of marketing case studies from innovative ED pros.

Prioritization of General Activities 1

"Things which matter most must never be at the mercy of things which matter least."

- Johann Wolfgang von Goethe

The top general activity priorities for EDOs are business attraction, retention, and expansion. All were chosen by roughly three quarters of respondents. After those three choices, there was a substantial drop, followed by entrepreneurial, community, and workforce development, and then marketing.

Figure 1-1. Prioritization of economic development staff time (percent indicating activity as top-5 priority)

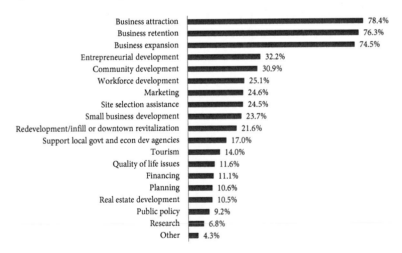

Business retention moved up slightly from when we last asked EDOs about their priorities. This is actually quite significant; business retention was the only general activity with a higher percentage in the most recent survey, as we added quite a few more options for EDOs that spread around the responses. The increased focus on business retention speaks to the challenges local businesses are having in a difficult economy, the lack of expansion and relocation deals for ED pros to pursue, and the growing trend toward small business and entrepreneurial support.

Marketing Effectiveness

2

"We immediately become more effective when we decide to change ourselves rather than asking things to change for us."

– Stephen Covey

Websites were again rated the most effective marketing strategy in the recent survey, with 82% of ED pros saying they are an effective means of marketing communities. After websites, the most highly rated strategies were out-of-town meetings, site selection consultants and familiarization tours, and public relations.

Table 2-1. Percent of ED pros rating marketing strategy effective, 2007-2011.

Marketing Strategy	2007	2009	2011
Website	79%	71%	82%
Out-of-Town Meetings	72%	56%	74%
Site Selection Consultants and Fam Tours	64%	49%	68%
Public Relations	64%	53%	65%
Special Events	56%	50%	60%
E-Mail	48%	45%	50%
Social Media	*	34%	47%
Targeted Lead Development Databases	43%	33%	42%
Trade Shows and Conferences	36%	32%	42%
Slogans, Logo and Graphic Identity	38%	29%	41%
Online Videos (YouTube, etc.)	*	22%	32%
Online Advertising	13%	18%	31%
Company Blog	*	15%	21%
Brochures	20%	18%	21%
Direct Mail	26%	14%	19%
Print Advertising	16%	11%	17%
TV/Radio Advertising	10%	11%	11%
Videos (VHS, DVD, etc)	14%	10%	10%
Telemarketing	6%	6%	5%

*was not a choice in 2007

There has been little change over the last four years in the order of these rankings, though the sentiments towards marketing in general have fluctuated markedly over the same time period, which included the Great Recession that began at the end of 2008. When surveyed in 2009 after the market crashed, their opinions had soured on just about every strategy. However, by 2011, the perceived effectiveness of marketing strategies rebounded, in most cases to higher levels than in 2007. Generally, the most highly rated strategies in 2007 (websites, out of town meetings, and site selection consultants/familiarization tours) were looked upon even more favorably by 2011. Only a couple of the lower rated strategies, notably direct mail and hard copy videos (VHS, DVD) dropped in perceived effectiveness from 2007 to 2011.

Online advertising had a very dramatic rise in perceived effectiveness over this time period, even avoiding the dip in 2009 that occurred for just about every other strategy. According to Nielsen, consumer trust in online search and display advertising rose from 2007 to 2011, prompting their global head of advertising to suggest that marketers should have "increased confidence in putting more of their ad dollars into this medium."[1]

Figure 2-1. How do you rate the effectiveness of your overall marketing programs and techniques?

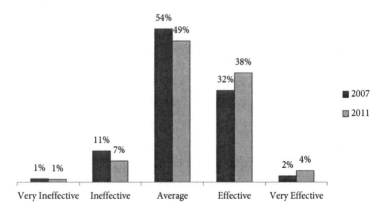

The recent optimism of EDOs extends to how they view their marketing programs as a whole. In 2011, EDOs were more likely to rate their programs as very effective or effective, and less likely to rate themselves average or ineffective. You will see later that we have used this question to see how the self-reported effective marketers behave differently from those that described their marketing programs as either average or ineffective.

Surf and Turf Marketing

The most effective marketing strategies ranked in the survey fall under the umbrella of "surf and turf" marketing. To succeed, EDOs must be increasingly high-tech and high-touch. The high-tech surfing is happening on the Internet and the high-touch turf relationships come from deeply connecting with people and companies.[2]

The high-tech strategies such as website, email, and social media lead to opportunities to develop high-touch personal relationships that foster economic growth in communities. Other high-touch strategies such as out-of-town meetings, fam tours, and special events include face-to-face time that develops personal connections with prospective investors.

Budgeting

3

"Don't tell me where your priorities are. Show me where you spend your money and I'll tell you what they are."

- James W. Frick, Former Vice President for Public Relations, Alumni Affairs, and Development, University of Notre Dame

Budgets for EDOs vary greatly. Understandably, the larger the area, the more funding the EDO will likely get, but the survey showed that EDOs serving larger areas also tended to spend a greater share of their total budgets on marketing. EDOs serving areas with 1 million to 5 million people spent 14% of their budgets on marketing, compared to EDOs serving areas with 10,000 to 25,000 people, which only allocated 5% of their budget to marketing.

Table 3-1. Median EDO marketing budget by population of the area served

Population	Median Marketing Budget	Marketing as % of Total Budget
Under 10,000	$12,500	6%
10,000 to 25,000	$8,250	5%
25,001 to 50,000	$25,000	10%
50,001 to 100,000	$25,515	6%
100,001 to 250,000	$50,000	9%
250,001 to 500,000	$85,000	9%
500,001 to 750,000	$120,000	10%
750,001 to 1 million	$76,000	8%
1 million to 5 million	$300,000	14%
Over 5 million	$100,000	3%

The median budget for EDOs was $500,000 and the median budget designated for marketing was $35,000. However, because the size of the population served impacts the budget, to benchmark your

EDO it makes more sense to compare to the median budget of your population group, rather than the median for all EDOs.

The table below compares the effectiveness ratings of marketing strategies to the budgets allocated for them. Websites received the highest budget share and enjoyed the highest effectiveness rating. Trade shows/conferences and out-of-town meetings with businesses both made slight gains in budget allocation to claim the 2nd and 3rd places on this list. Previously, those rankings were held by print advertising and brochures, so this shift represents an increasing emphasis on personal contact as well as the decreasing importance of printed materials.

Table 3-2. Average budget allocation vs. perceived effectiveness

Marketing Strategy	Average Budget Allocation	Rating Effective	Change from 2007
Website	17%	82%	**
Trade Shows and Conferences	12%	42%	↑
Out-of-Town Meetings with Businesses	10%	74%	**
Print Advertising	10%	17%	↓
Brochures	9%	21%	↓
Special Events	8%	60%	**
Public Relations	8%	65%	**
Site Selection Consultants and Fam Tours	6%	68%	**
E-Mail	5%	50%	**
Direct Mail	3%	19%	↓
Online Advertising	3%	31%	↑
Slogans, Logo and Graphic Identity	3%	41%	**
Targeted Lead Development Databases	2%	42%	**
TV/Radio Advertising	2%	11%	**
Social Media	2%	47%	*
Online Videos (YouTube, etc.)	1%	32%	*
Videos (VHS, DVD, etc)	1%	10%	**
Company Blog	0%	21%	*
Telemarketing	0%	5%	**

*was not a choice in 2007
**change was less than one percent

Three of the top five marketing categories in terms of budget share had relatively low ratings for effectiveness: trade shows/conferences, print advertising, and brochures. While the budget share for trade shows increased from 2007 to 2011, the budget allocations for print advertising and brochures decreased the most of any strategies from

2007 to 2011 except direct mail, which indicates that EDOs are scaling down printed material marketing activities that don't work as well as other strategies (perhaps because they all read our last book!). Even so, the budget allotments for these strategies are still quite high given their low effectiveness ratings. They warrant more scrutiny and are discussed in more detail in the following sections.

Trade Shows and Conferences

A 2005 study by the Brookings Institution found that even as cities race to construct bigger and better convention centers to take advantage of what had been perceived as a burgeoning market, attendance at the 200 largest trade show events remained at the same level as in 1993. Some cities, including some of the most historically successful convention areas, have experienced declines of over 50% in convention attendance since the late 1990s when attendance was peaking. The authors point out that the decline is not simply due to business shifting from one city to another or the restructuring of certain trade events, but also to "industry consolidation, reductions in business travel in the face of increasing cost and difficulty, and alternative means of conveying and gathering information."[3]

The exhibition industry suffered greatly during the recession. Each year, the Center for Exhibition Industry Research publishes an index that measures the performance of the industry based on net square feet of exhibit space sold, professional attendees, and total event gross revenue. In 2009, the index fell 12.5%, which was four times the size of the decline in 2008, the largest previous loss. The index fell a third straight year in 2010, after which it rebounded 2.7% in 2011.[4] The exhibition industry's recent performance shows some strength, as it outperformed real GDP growth by 1%, though it still has a long climb to get back to its stature pre-recession. The rise of web conferencing does reduce the necessity of conference travel, and certainly poses questions for the long-term future of trade shows.

Print Advertising

The decline of print media has accelerated so rapidly in the past few years that many longstanding newspapers have been forced to shut down their daily print operations and move online, including *the Seattle Post-Intelligencer* and *the Times-Picayune* in New Orleans. A blog entry reposted in *the Atlantic* showed that revenue from newspaper advertisements has plummeted from $60 billion in the 1990s to only $20 billion in 2011,[5] and *Forbes* reported that online ad revenues were set to surpass print ad revenues in 2012.[6] To ironically emphasize this new reality, Google recently placed an ad in Canada's *Globe and Mail* newspaper that read "You know who needs a haircut? People searching for a haircut…Maybe that's why ads on Google work."[7]

The decline in advertising within the site location magazine industry is more moribund and is illustrated in Figure 3-1, which shows ad pages declining in every site location magazine from 2005 to 2010. Ad revenue has also been declining (see Figure C-1 in Appendix).

Two of the leading publications for the site location industry have ceased print publication within the past few years: *Plants, Sites & Parks* in 2004 and *Expansion Management* in 2008. Among the remaining audited magazines, *Area Development* has gone from first to last place and is at a level of advertising pages lower than when the other two magazines went out of business. *Site Selection* is in first place with relatively strong performance. *Business Facilities*' audience of companies in the growing service industries has differentiated the magazine compared to the others, which focus more distribution in the manufacturing industry.

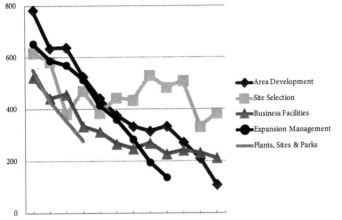

Figure 3-1. Total Annual Ad Pages for Site Location Magazines, 1999-2010

Source: Inquiry Management Systems. No data for Plants, Sites & Parks was available after 2002, nor for Expansion Management after 2007.

Brochures

A brochure can summarize the positive attributes that a community wants to advertise into a tangible, take-away package. Glossy brochures, regardless of their contents, can impress an audience by hinting at the dedication and resources of a community necessary to put such packages together. Historically, brochures and business cards have also been used as a physical expression that serves to legitimize a person and/or organization. However, since the production of brochures is receiving a significant budget allocation by ED pros but receives one of the lowest effectiveness ratings, it raises doubt about the value of continuing this marketing practice. An influential corporate real estate site selector commented that they do not have much purpose other than proving that the organization exists. According to Bob Ady, "Brochures establish credibility, but serve little purpose otherwise."[8]

Brochures are often very general, trying to appeal to many audiences at once. A 2000 economic development study from the University of North Texas found that marketing activities "are increasingly conducted through the introduction of specific products and promotion of economic niches rather than exclusively with glossy brochures and trade shows."[9] The study also found that newer marketing approaches have been affected by national and subnational budget shortfalls since the 1970s, which have made communities rethink the use of expensive strategies like brochures.

This was our first survey in which EDOs were asked about their use of social media. While only receiving the 15th highest budget allocation, social media received the 7th highest effectiveness rating. EDOs seem to be finding that social media can be very effective even when they don't spend much on it.

We also asked EDOs whether they were planning to increase or decrease funding for their marketing strategies in the next five years. Over 70% of EDOs anticipated that they would increase their spending on websites in the next 5 years. The only other marketing strategy for which the majority of EDOs planned to increase spending was social media. The strategies most likely to be cut were print advertising, telemarketing, and TV/radio advertising. Of all the activities that EDOs engage in, marketing experiences the most budget volatility. In a short survey we performed in 2009 at the depths of the economic slump, marketing was the general activity most likely to be cut from EDO budgets as well as the activity most likely to be increased (see Table C-1 in Appendix).

Table 3-2. Largest anticipated increases in marketing budgets

Marketing Strategy	Anticipating Increase in Next 5 Years	Anticipating Decrease in Next 5 Years
Website	70%	2%
Social Media	51%	6%
Site Selection Consultants and Fam Tours	45%	11%
Out-of-Town Meetings with Businesses	44%	13%
Special Events	40%	10%
Public Relations	40%	10%
E-Mail	39%	5%
Online Videos (YouTube, etc.)	35%	12%
Online Advertising	34%	15%
Targeted Lead Development Databases	33%	15%
Trade Shows and Conferences	30%	20%
Slogans, Logo and Graphic Identity	26%	15%
Company Blog	23%	14%
Print Advertising	12%	43%
Brochures	11%	34%
Direct Mail	11%	35%
Videos (VHS, DVD, etc)	11%	38%
TV/Radio Advertising	9%	39%
Telemarketing	7%	41%

Jonathan Bittner, Director of Business and Economic Development at Anchorage Economic Development Corporation, says "we've moved from a print driven approach to an entirely electronic marketing and outreach strategy over the last year. It's much cheaper to produce and send out than printed content: no postage, no printing costs, no paper, etc. especially if you can do the design in-house."[10]

Of the top five most funded marketing strategies, three of them were rated effective by less than half of respondents: trade shows/conferences, print advertising, and brochures. One would think that EDOs would plan to rectify this situation by decreasing funding for those ineffective strategies in the future, giving them a budget share more in line with their actual worth. As might be expected, EDOs planned cuts to funding for print advertising and brochures more than they planned increases. Trade shows/conferences was the only strategy of the three for which EDOs planned to increase funding more than they planned to cut funding. Perhaps EDOs think they have to add more money to get better results with trade shows and conferences, or they may not be aware that, in general, this strategy has a lower return on investment than other high-budget strategies. Another possibility is that ED pros enjoy conferences, travel, and the opportunities for professional development that they offer, so they include this in the budget for personal benefit. Or perhaps EDOs are just going to the wrong shows.

Online Advertising

ED pros were prescient in their plans to increase budget allocations in online advertising since the first survey. Online advertising budgets grew the most of any marketing strategy since the first survey. Also, online advertising was unique among all marketing strategies because it was the only one that had an effectiveness rating increase in both the 2009 and 2011 surveys.

While it has risen recently, still only 3% of economic development marketing budgets is allocated toward online advertising, and only 31% of respondents identified it as an effective strategy. This is dramatically different from the trends occurring in the larger US market of companies. North American firms allocate 18% of their marketing budgets to online advertising, roughly six times what economic development organizations spend, and this share is rising (see Figure C-2 in Appendix).[11] Figure 3-2 maps the growth of online advertising revenues over the past ten years, during which time the compound annual growth rate was 20.3%. Even after the dot-com bust at the end of 2000, the much publicized decline in Internet advertising was actually only a small dip. By 2004, Internet advertising had surpassed its peak from the dot-com hey-day. Internet advertising's annual growth rate has been higher than all other media in each year since 2005, and since 2005 it has surpassed the market revenue share of cable television, newspapers, and radio (see Figure C-3 in Appendix).[12] Online advertising is growing because it works. Top level executives, according to Invesp Consulting, agree that online advertising provides the highest return on investment.[13]

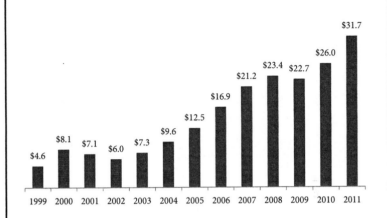

Figure 3-2. Annual internet advertising revenue, in billions

Source: *PricewaterhouseCoopers/Interactive Advertising Bureau*

ED pros are lagging behind a strong online advertising movement. In a discussion that came out of a training at the Southern Economic Development Council, many participants were confused and inquisitive as to why ED pros are not investing in online advertising at the same rate as EDOs were investing in their websites. When asked about their own behavior, however, it was discovered that only a few in the room used Google AdWords, the most popular online keyword pay-per-click advertising tool. One of the key reasons explained as to why they were not using this service was because they didn't know how to use it.[14] Online advertising presents an opportunity for ED pros to invest in a growing marketing trend not recognized or used by many competing EDOs.

Industry Targeting and Scope

4

"The odds of hitting your target go up dramatically when you aim at it."

– Mal Pancoast

Any marketing program needs a clearly defined audience. An EDO should define the reach of its audience in terms of both geography and range of industries.

Survey respondents tended to represent organizations that were at the city or county level. Only 3% were larger than statewide organizations. When asked to describe the geographic scope of their marketing efforts, however, the most frequent response was global at 30%, followed by nationwide at 23%. Clearly, the average EDO is responding to the forces of globalization and expanding the size of its target market area far outside the boundaries of its service area.

Figure 4-1. EDO service area vs. target market area

What is the area served by your organization?

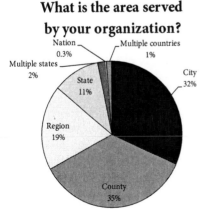

What is the geographic scope of your marketing efforts?

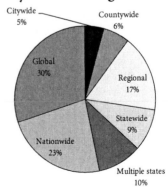

EDOs often target specific industries to attract and grow in their communities. In the survey, ED pros were asked to pick the top five industries that they target. The table below shows which industries were chosen the most. For comparison's sake, we asked site selectors and corporate real estate professionals to tell us the five industries for which they most needed to locate space, whose answers are also included.

Table 4-1. Industries targeted most by EDOs

Industry	Targeted by EDOs	Served by Site Selectors
Manufacturing - advanced	44%	24%
Manufacturing - alternative energy/renewable energy	41%	17%
Manufacturing - traditional	36%	36%
Distribution/wholesale trade	30%	36%
Information technology/high-technology	29%	27%
Entrepreneurial businesses	27%	11%
Aerospace/aviation	25%	12%
Healthcare	24%	18%
Biotechnology	21%	15%
Retail	21%	22%

In our last survey, the overwhelming favorite industry of ED pros was manufacturing. Because manufacturing is such a broad industry, we wanted to determine what subsectors of manufacturing were most desirable, so we broke down manufacturing into three categories: advanced (pharmaceuticals, medical devices, etc.), alternative energy/renewable energy, and traditional (auto, steel, oil, gas, etc.). These subsectors were ranked one, two, and three by ED pros, so clearly it is not just one aspect of manufacturing that communities are looking for.

The continued dominance of manufacturing in economic development is notable in light of the overall decline of the manufacturing sector, which has lost 20% of its jobs from 2004 to 2010 (See Figure 4-2). This priority may be due to the political concerns in communities of keeping high-paying blue collar jobs in the midst of the national transformation to a service economy. It should be noted, however, that declining employment does not equate to a dying industry. "Manufacturing employment has fallen and will likely continue to fall, but that does not mean investment will continue to fall," says Mark Sweeney of McCallum Sweeney. "For manufacturing to be competitive, it must be efficient with capital investments that are labor-saving. The investment to job ratio has increased. It is not unusual to have $1 million in investment per job, roughly double the ratio of ten years ago."[15]

Figure 4-2. U.S. Employment Growth in Selected Industries, 2004-2010

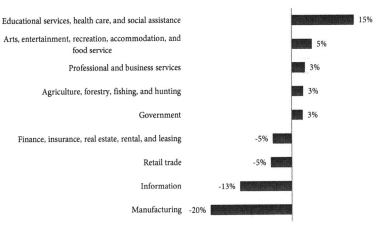

Source: Bureau of Economic Analysis

While site selectors did not find themselves serving the newer branches of manufacturing (advanced manufacturing and alternative energy), their prioritization of traditional manufacturing lined up with ED pros. Clearly, traditional manufacturing is not dead. The newer, burgeoning sectors of manufacturing are not high priorities of site selectors now, but we have spoken with many site selectors who indicate that these newer sectors will become a greater part of what site selectors service.

Many site selectors personally interviewed were hopeful about the future of manufacturing in the United States. "You look at the statistics and it's still by far the most active sector [for site selection consultants]," says Deane Foote of Foote Consulting Group, "overall it still has more projects than any other sector. Even though you read about it all going overseas, it's just not true."[16] The nature of manufacturing in the United States is certainly changing. "Low-cost manufacturing will continue to leave North America," explains Don Schjeldahl of the Austin Company, "but what's happening is that new technologies are leading to new markets, and a lot of these technologies require sophisticated manufacturing, customization, time sensitive manufacturing, or all those things, and you need highly skilled people."[17] Many site selectors interviewed pointed to alternative energy as a key source of new investment. Even many traditional manufacturers are realizing the benefits of staying local, such as just-in-time shipping. Dennis Donovan of the Wadley Donovan Group says that freight sensitive businesses, such as battery manufacturers, are expanding less overseas due to high transportation costs.[18] He explained that within the United States, manufacturing is locating in smaller communities because of lower operating and labor costs.

Site location is also a far more important decision for manufacturers than for most other industries. "Unlike retailers who can locate on every corner, manufacturers only site a new facility once in a great while," says Tim Monger of Colliers International. "There's more at stake for manufacturing than for any other industry, because they're investing a significant amount of money. It's quite a roll of the dice in setting up a new location and making sure you have a good location and labor pool."[19]

For site selectors, the industry they most often served was corporate headquarters at 44%, which was only targeted by 18% of ED pros (the list of industries most serviced by site selectors can be found in Table C-2 in the Appendix). Call centers, finance/insurance, and business services also were far more of a priority for site selectors than for ED pros. Among site selectors themselves, site selection consultants were more likely to serve manufacturing-related industries, including food processing and aerospace. Corporate real estate professionals, on the other hand, were more likely to serve industries in the service sector, such as IT, retail, finance, healthcare, and education.[20]

For EDOs that work with site selectors, this variation is important, as site selectors may not be focused on the same priorities of EDOs.

The EDOs that target industries such as alternative energy manufacturing, aerospace, healthcare, and biotech may need to target these industries directly, work with corporate real estate pros serving these companies, or identify site selectors that do work in these industries.

Table 4-2. Industries targeted by effective versus ineffective marketers

Industry	Effective Marketers	Ineffective Marketers	Difference
Aerospace/aviation	37%	20%	17%
Corporate headquarters	25%	15%	10%
Information technology/high-technology	35%	26%	10%

Looking at the largest differences in industry targeting between effective marketers and ineffective marketers, effective marketers were much more likely to target aerospace/aviation, corporate headquarters, and information technology. The emphasis on corporate headquarters makes a lot of sense, as they provide enormous value to communities in many ways, including tax dollars generated, the location of high-paid managerial employees, and the name recognition that can be used to attract additional companies. Site selectors also service this industry more than any other, so it indicates that corporations are still looking for new locations. The other two industries both represent technical sectors that require a very skilled workforce, an asset that effective marketers may feel more confident they will be able to provide.

Location and Organization Directories

5

Directories of Economic Development Organizations

Within the past few years, a growing number of economic development directory listing services have sprouted. Over two-thirds of our respondents indicated that they had created listings in these directories. 12% were not aware of these services.

Figure 5-1. Have you created a listing for your organization in any online economic development directories?

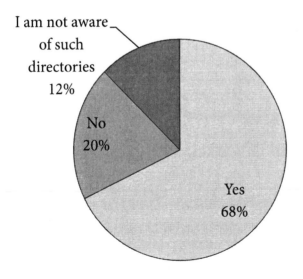

I am not aware of such directories 12%

No 20%

Yes 68%

Location Directories

A few nationwide location directories exist that aid site selectors and businesses in finding space to locate and expand. Another recent survey of site selectors performed by *Business Facilities* magazine found that 53% of executives utilize such directories when making a location decision.[21] When asked which features of these directories were highly important, 60% wanted contact information, 53% wanted information on available properties, and 45% stressed the importance of market data.

Examples of economic development and location directories include, but are not limited to:

www.ecodevdirectory.com
www.zoomprospector.com
www.businessfacilities.com
www.siteselection.com
www.bxjmag.com

There are also regional and statewide directories that are provided through economic development membership associations.

How Site Selectors Get Information

6

"To be successful and grow your business and revenues, you must match the way you market your products with the way your prospects learn about and shop for your products."
- Brian Halligan, Co-Author, *Inbound Marketing*

For economic development organizations working with site selectors,[22] it is important to understand the behavior of these professionals.[23] How and when site selectors obtain information about communities matters. The results of our separate, parallel national survey shows that when researching communities, the top sources of information for site selectors and corporate real estate professionals are brokers and EDO websites. While EDOs may have limited influence over brokers, they most certainly can influence their own websites.

Figure 6-1. Prior to personally contacting an EDO to let them know you are considering their community, you typically gather information about communities from:

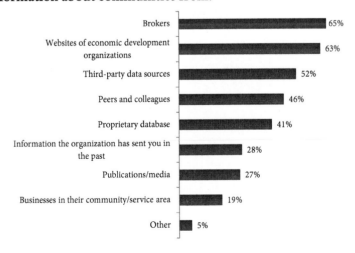

Different types of respondents gathered information differently. Corporate real estate professionals were more likely to gather their information from brokers (26% compared to 8% of site selection consultants), while site selection consultants placed greater emphasis on third-party data sources and proprietary databases, as can be seen in Figure C-4 in the Appendix.

Contact with Economic Development Organizations

We asked site selectors when, during the site selection process, they would first visit an EDO's website, as well as when they would first contact a staff person at the EDO. In the first two phases of site selection, site selectors were considerably more likely to visit an EDO website than to contact an EDO. This was very similar to what we saw in 2007.

Figure 6-2. Timing of contacts (cumulative) made by site selectors

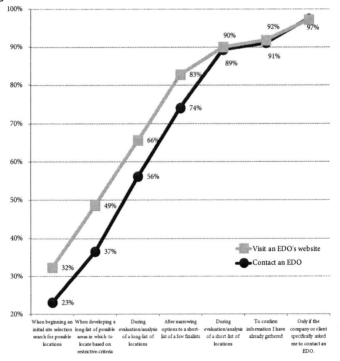

Corporate real estate professionals are considerably more likely to visit EDO websites in the first couple stages of the site selection process, though more site selection consultants visit EDO websites at some point during the site selection process. The same trends are true for contacting EDOs.

Figure 6-3. When would you first visit an economic development organization's website?

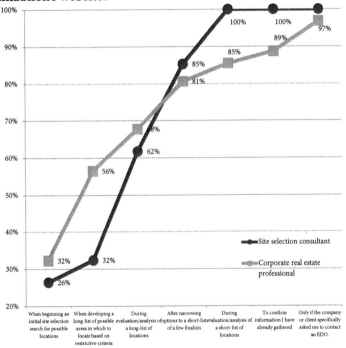

By the end of the second stage of site selection (developing a long-list of possible areas), site selectors were 33% more likely to have visited economic development organization websites than to have personally contacted an organization. This represents a significant advantage for EDOs that provide the type of information that is desired and that can help them get through to the next phase of site selection evaluation, as the farther along they get in the process, the more likely they will have an opportunity to personally persuade the decision. Michael Henderson, Vice President of Rockwood Real Estate Advisors, a real estate firm in New York City, recently commented that "You pretty much can't do an effective site search without ED websites."[24]

Many communities and EDOs are being eliminated from the site selection process before they are ever contacted, which indicates the extreme importance of an effective website. One survey respondent from 2007 wrote:

> *"We often get calls from businesses that are already past the early state of their decision making process because they use our website tools to help them with their analysis. Because of our website our staff now spends more time with qualified and educated businesses instead of people that are just asking simple questions when they aren't even sure if they are going to invest in our community. For example, one business called and I started asking him basic questions and telling him about our community. He said, 'I know that stuff. I saw it on your website. I want you to set up a tour for me of three buildings that match what I need that I found on your website.'"*

97% of site selectors use the websites of economic development organizations at some point in their research. At the same time, the same percentage reported personally contacting an economic development organization at some point during the site selection process. Even in a time where more and more work is being automated, the survey results show that the services of ED pros are still indispensable. "Economic development organizations still comprise the lifeblood of site selection," says Dennis Donovan. "Once we're down to 10 or 15 potential locations per project, we reach out to economic development organizations before we have to visit local areas to find local operating conditions, such as what are the expanding companies, water and sewer capacity, electric power reliability, etc."[25]

Bob Ady, the site selection pioneer who passed away this year, once wrote that "the site selection consultant uses the information from a community's website and other online sources. If a community doesn't have a website, the website cannot easily be found or it doesn't have the right type of information, the consultant moves on to other communities that have the information he or she needs."

In addition to the ease of obtaining information via the web, the often confidential nature of site selection decision-making gives the site selector further incentive for minimizing personal contact with the EDO in the early stages of the site selection process. A community that does not maintain a user-friendly website thus runs the risk of being eliminated from a location search without being given the chance to interact with the site selector personally. In such situations, the EDO would not even be aware that they could have been under consideration and that they might have helped their cause had they provided enough information online for a site selector to further the location search process in their community.

Website Features

7

"In today's information age of marketing and Web 2.0, a company's website is the key to their entire business."
-Marcus Sheridan, Author of The Sales Lion Blog

When asked to rate the importance of features on a website, there was a veritable dead heat for first place between land/sites and buildings inventory, labor force, and demographic reports. This was not a change from our last survey. Since our last survey, the biggest gains were made for business assistance services, which may reflect a growing emphasis on entrepreneurial support within the field.

Table 7-1. Most important features in an economic development website

Website Feature	% EDOs Rating Feature Important	Change from 2007
Land/sites and buildings inventory	91%	↑
Labor force	91%	**
Demographic reports	90%	**
Infrastructure	86%	↑
Maps	85%	↓
Major industries or business/industry clusters	83%	↓
Staff directory and contact information	83%	↓
Incentives	81%	↑
Major employers	80%	**
GIS mapping tools for site selection analysis assistance	77%	↑
Business assistance services	74%	↑
Quality of life	73%	↓
Employment training programs	70%	↓
Testimonials and success stories	67%	↑
Hyperlinks to other organizations	67%	↓
News about community	60%	↓
Social media integration	60%	*
Comparisons to other areas	55%	**
Business list	53%	↑
Formatting option for mobile devices/mobile apps	51%	*
Transactions	48%	↑
Videos	33%	↑
User-generated content	24%	↑

*was not a choice in 2007
**change was less than one percent

The table above lists what EDOs think is important, but that can be different from what they actually have. Figure 7-1 shows both what ED pros have and what they plan to add within 2-5 years. Most EDOs have staff directory and contact information, hyperlinks, demographics, and maps.

This data also shows what will be the fastest growing website features that EDOs will add in the next few years. Topping the list is mobile formatting, followed by GIS site selection analysis, social media, and testimonials. Although some of these aren't implemented on many websites now, a large percentages of EDOs plan to add them soon.

Figure 7-1. Which website features do you have?

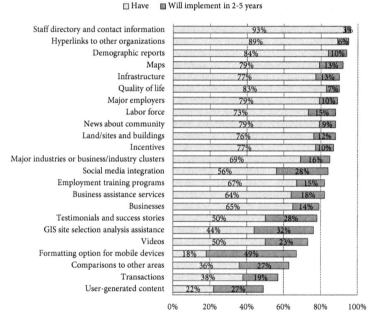

□ Have ▨ Will implement in 2-5 years

Feature	Have	Will implement in 2-5 years
Staff directory and contact information	93%	3%
Hyperlinks to other organizations	89%	6%
Demographic reports	84%	10%
Maps	79%	13%
Infrastructure	77%	13%
Quality of life	83%	7%
Major employers	79%	10%
Labor force	73%	15%
News about community	79%	9%
Land/sites and buildings	76%	12%
Incentives	77%	10%
Major industries or business/industry clusters	69%	16%
Social media integration	56%	28%
Employment training programs	67%	15%
Business assistance services	64%	18%
Businesses	65%	14%
Testimonials and success stories	50%	28%
GIS site selection analysis assistance	44%	32%
Videos	50%	23%
Formatting option for mobile devices	18%	49%
Comparisons to other areas	36%	27%
Transactions	38%	19%
User-generated content	22%	27%

We also looked at what separates the EDOs that report their marketing to be effective from those that do not in terms of their websites. The effective marketers were a lot more likely to include comparisons to other areas, business lists, and geographic information system (GIS) site selection analysis.

Table 7-2. Which website features do you have? (effective versus ineffective marketers)

Website Items	Effective Marketers	Ineffective Marketers	Difference
Comparisons to other areas	51%	27%	23%
Business list	78%	57%	21%
GIS site selection analysis assistance	56%	37%	19%
Testimonials and success stories	62%	43%	19%
Major industries or business/industry clusters	81%	63%	18%
Videos	61%	43%	18%

Website visitors now often expect to access information interactively and dynamically, rather than by opening an Adobe Acrobat file or a static report on a webpage. Our most recent survey shows that a growing number of EDOs see that interactivity is important when presenting a sites and buildings inventory, maps, demographic reports, incentives, or lists of businesses and industries.

Figure 7-2. How important is it to have the following items be interactive?

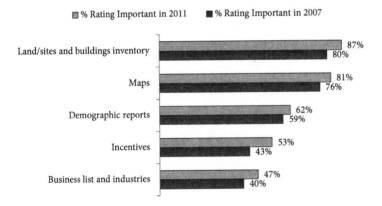

Back in 2007, we asked whether EDOs display their maps, properties, and demographic reports in a static format, or whether they made their sites truly interactive using a geographic information system (GIS). The data projected that GIS would be at a tipping point in 2-5 years, as the amount of people that planned to add interactive features was greater than the amount that had these interactive features at the time. 81% of site selectors feel that GIS technology would be helpful to them when using economic development websites, up 4% from 2007 (see Figure C-5 in Appendix).

Consistent with the forecasts of the previous survey, the addition of interactive maps and site selection GIS analysis assistance is now at a tipping point in which nearly the majority of EDOs have this technology. In the next few years, the minority that does not have it will be at an online service disadvantage.

Figure 7-3. Interactive features on economic development websites

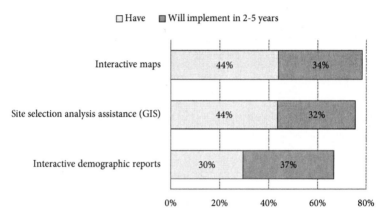

EDOs are now much more likely to include analytics on their websites for visitor tracking. Back in 2007, 29% of EDOs said they did not track visitors to their websites, and now that figure is down to 2%. EDOs are also more likely now to use analytics services designed specifically for the economic development industry, as is further discussed in Christopher Finn's case study on Buffalo Niagara's Commercial Listing System in the final chapter.

Figure 7-4. How do you track visitors to your website?

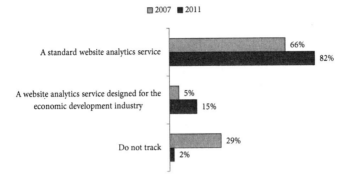

The data shows that EDOs are actually less active now when it comes to updating the content on their websites than they were in 2007 (see Figure C-6 in Appendix). However, when looking at the numbers for 2011, EDOs that reported themselves to have effective marketing were far more likely to update their websites in a timely fashion. 19% of effective marketers reported that they updated their websites on a daily basis, versus only 8% of ineffective marketers. You can see as you go down the chart that the three choices representing the most frequent updating schedules were dominated by effective marketers, whereas the choices representing the most lax updating schedules were all dominated by ineffective marketers.

Figure 7-5. How often is your website updated?

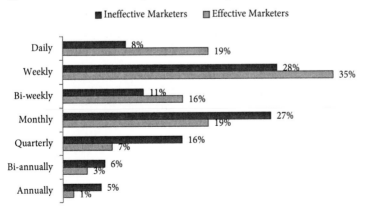

Social Media

8

"Institutions that once had to go through media to deliver information are now themselves media."

— Andrew Machison, Founder, We Media

Social media is still a relatively new means of communication. However, it is important for ED pros to recognize its importance, as social media is playing an increasingly large role for communication in the business community. The Center for Marketing Research at the University of Massachusetts Dartmouth has reported for the past 5 years on social media usage among the 500 fastest-growing U.S. private companies, collectively recognized by *Inc. Magazine* as the Inc. 500. Of the 170 Inc. 500 companies for 2011 that responded to the Center's latest survey, 74% used Facebook, 73% used LinkedIn, and 64% used Twitter.[26] EDOs should be keenly aware of what emerging technologies are popular among the business community, and, in this vein, any EDO that wants to reach the business community should make use of social media.

Unlike some of the more traditional means of mass communication, such as direct mail and print media, social media often blurs the line between professional and personal worlds in ways that traditional means of mass communication have not. For instance, a staff member for a chamber of commerce that is working to create a brochure to mail out to the local business community likely would not be tempted during that process to create a brochure to send to their friends detailing their plans for the weekend at the same time. However, it is entirely likely that the same staff member, during one five minute session on Twitter, would be updating the chamber's membership on an upcoming event, checking to see what others have said about the chamber, and at the same time interacting with other colleagues and friends about matters both personal and professional.

While there is often some gray area, we wanted to differentiate between these two worlds when asking ED pros about social media. First, we asked which social media strategies they engaged in for personal use. The most commonly used site was Facebook with a whopping 81% of respondents reporting use. This is not surprising, as ED pros are a social bunch and they generally embrace ways to connect with others. 74% used LinkedIn for reasons outside of their own job, which indicates that most ED pros are likely proactive about seeking to further their career by networking to find other opportunities.

Figure 8-1. Which of the following social media platforms do you engage in for personal use outside of work?

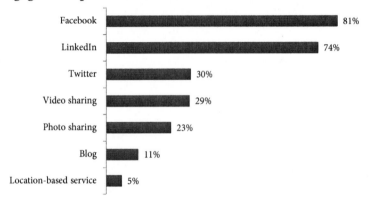

We also asked which social media strategies the company engaged in, regardless of whether the respondent was involved in the execution. The most popular platform for an EDO was the Facebook Page, with 73% of organizations taking part. This is high, but it is smaller than the percentage of ED pros using Facebook. Some of our respondents that are familiar with Facebook could most likely help their EDOs to set up organizational Facebook Pages.[27]

It is interesting to note that while only 30% of respondents used Twitter personally, 58% reported that their organization possesses a Twitter account. Clearly Twitter has come a long way. While it may have had a reputation in its early days as a venue for people to share mundane details of their personal lives, it has become a very effective means of communicating timely information about an organization or community's activities, and is now embraced by the majority of EDOs.

Figure 8-2. Does your organization engage in the following social media strategies?

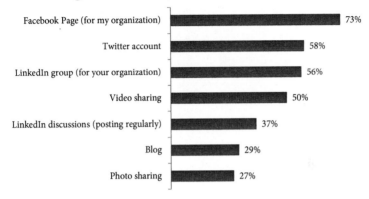

When asked to rate which communication strategies for economic development were most effective, ED pros gave the highest ratings to LinkedIn, followed by Facebook, video sharing, and Twitter. These effectiveness ratings are considerably lower than the percentages of EDOs that engage in them, so even though EDOs that use a social platform are more likely to rate it effective (see Figure C-8 in Appendix), there is certainly still some skepticism about the effectiveness of these channels among organizations that are engaging in them. We should keep in mind when looking at these results that we are still at an early adoption stage.[28] As EDOs become more comfortable and proficient in these strategies, and as the business community's involvement on these platforms grows, we expect EDOs to have more success with social media.

Figure 8-3. Percent of ED pros rating social media channel as an effective marketing strategy for economic development

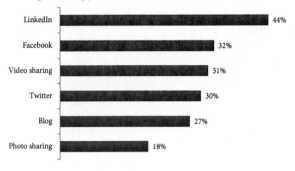

It is not enough to create a social media account. To get any real benefit out of a social media presence, it is important to engage frequently and make use of its real time nature. 20% of ED pros used Facebook and Twitter on a daily basis, and 15% used LinkedIn daily. There is a good amount of variation among the types of respondents, however, as ED pros that rated their marketing programs as effective were more likely to use social media platforms daily than those who did not. They were twice as likely to use Facebook on a daily basis, and 12% more likely to use Twitter daily. More information on social media usage can be found in the next chapter, which shows how the survey results varied by different characteristics of the EDOs.

Figure 8-4. Percent of ED pros using social media channels on at least a daily basis

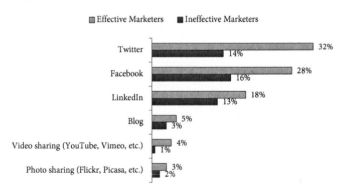

In our separate survey of site selectors, 61% of respondents agreed that social media will grow in importance in their jobs in the coming years, though only a quarter said that they have used social media for research during the site selection process. In comparing the surveys, site selectors spent an average of 23 minutes per day engaging with social media compared to 26 minutes per day from ED pros. However, not every platform was dominated by ED pros. 35% of site selectors said they used LinkedIn on a daily basis, compared to only 15% of ED pros (see Figure C-8 in Appendix). EDOs would do well to be active on the same platforms used by the site selectors they are trying to reach.

Variation by Size, Region, and Structure

9

"Hawaii is a unique state...it is different from the other 49 states. Well, all states are different, but it's got a particularly unique situation."

— Dan Quayle

There is no one way to do economic development; one size does not fit all. Here we will look at some of the patterns in economic development marketing based on characteristics of the EDOs surveyed.

Organizational Structure

Government agencies were more spread out in their prioritization of general activities than EDCs. Both groups had the same top three priorities, though EDCs came to a stronger consensus on them. On the other hand, many government respondents chose redevelopment (40%) and tourism (21%) as top priorities, which barely registered for EDCs. The activity that EDCs chose in the greatest numbers over government agencies was marketing, with 29% of EDCs ranking it a top five priority compared to only 17% of government agencies. Marketing can be thought of as a support activity that complements or "markets" the other activities that an EDO engages in. Government agencies may be spread too thin on their primary activities that they don't have the resources to promote those activities through marketing to the same extent that EDCs can, which tend to be more focused in the types of activities in which EDCs engage.

Table 9-1. Prioritization of economic development staff time (percent indicating activity as top-5 priority)

General Activity	EDC	Government
Business attraction	84%	76%
Business expansion	82%	70%
Business retention	83%	77%
Community development	28%	34%
Entrepreneurial development	39%	30%
Financing	16%	13%
Marketing	**29%**	**17%**
Other	2%	3%
Planning	5%	17%
Public policy	4%	8%
Quality of life issues	11%	12%
Real estate development	13%	11%
Redevelopment/infill or downtown revitalization	9%	40%
Research	4%	4%
Site selection assistance	27%	19%
Small business development	23%	27%
Support local govt and econ dev agencies	9%	17%
Tourism	7%	21%
Workforce development	30%	21%

Government agencies and EDOs did not differ significantly in their marketing budgets, either in the size of their total budgets across all marketing strategies, or in how they allocated their marketing budgets across the various strategies. Regarding social media, even though both groups directed roughly the same budget share to social media, their activity levels were rather different. When asked how frequently they use various social media platforms, government agencies were significantly more likely to use Twitter and Facebook on a daily basis.

Figure 9-1. How active is your organization on the following social media platforms? (% indicating at least daily usage)

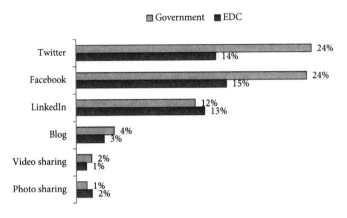

Population Size/Urbanity

We found that the smaller organizations tended to prioritize marketing more than the larger organizations.

Table 9-2. Prioritization of economic development staff time (percent indicating activity as top-5 priority)

General Activity	Less than 25,000	25,000 to 100,000	More than 100,000
Business attraction	77%	86%	76%
Business expansion	67%	79%	75%
Business retention	75%	86%	73%
Community development	51%	25%	28%
Entrepreneurial development	34%	31%	32%
Financing	8%	6%	14%
Marketing	**30%**	**26%**	**23%**
Other	3%	1%	6%
Planning	17%	7%	11%
Public policy	4%	6%	12%
Quality of life issues	23%	14%	8%
Real estate development	15%	12%	9%
Redevelopment/infill or downtown revitalization	33%	25%	17%
Research	2%	1%	11%
Site selection assistance	14%	26%	27%
Small business development	24%	23%	24%
Support local govt and econ dev agencies	10%	11%	22%
Tourism	32%	13%	10%
Workforce development	17%	26%	27%

Larger and more urban areas had a stronger orientation to targeting industries that create jobs for those in the knowledge economy, such as finance, science, and high-tech. As for manufacturing, the bigger and more urban the area, the more likely it is to target advanced manufacturing. This may have something to do with the kinds of talent needed to work in such facilities that may only be present in larger urban areas.

Rural areas were least likely to target advanced manufacturing, but most likely to target both traditional manufacturing (auto, steel, oil, etc.) and alternative energy. What remains of the remaining large-scale traditional manufacturing in this country has been increasingly concentrated in rural areas due to low land prices and transportation costs,[29] so even though that sector may be in decline, it makes sense that rural areas would try to retain that base. In addition, the strong prioritization of alternative energy in rural areas hints that these areas are also trying to find ways for the existing manufacturing labor pool to transition their skills to a more promising subsector of manufacturing.

Table 9-3. Industries targeted by urbanity of the service area (percent indicating industry at top 5 priority)

Industry	Urban	Suburban	Rural
Finance/insurance	14%	11%	3%
Information technology/high-technology	33%	32%	19%
Manufacturing - traditional (auto, steel, oil, gas, etc.)	27%	30%	44%
Manufacturing - advanced (pharma., med. devices, etc.)	44%	50%	32%
Manufacturing - alternative energy/renewable energy	31%	36%	47%
Sciences (and life sciences/biotech)	15%	12%	6%

Urban areas were considerably more active in their use of social media. EDOs from urban areas were the most likely to have a presence on each of the major social media strategies, and were most likely to use these same strategies on a daily basis. Rural areas lagged both urban and suburban areas on these measures.

Table 9-4. Social media platforms utilized by urbanity of the service area

Social Media Platform	Urban	Suburban	Rural
Facebook Page (for my organization)	84%	72%	65%
Twitter account	75%	60%	41%
Video sharing (YouTube, Vimeo, etc.)	60%	55%	37%
Photo sharing (Flickr, Picasa, etc.)	36%	22%	22%
LinkedIn group (for your organization)	68%	56%	48%
LinkedIn discussions (posting regularly)	48%	34%	28%
Blog	43%	26%	20%

Region

We categorized our respondents into four different regions based on the boundaries of the leading regional economic development membership associations.

Figure 9-2. Regional map

Similar to what we discovered in our last survey, accommodation/ food service, retail, and tourism were most heavily targeted by Western organizations, perhaps due to the need of EDOs in California to seek revenue from sales taxes when electoral measures have limited their ability to rely on revenues from property taxes. As for manufacturing, the Northeast was the most oriented around advanced manufacturing, the West around alternative energy, and the Midwest and South around traditional manufacturing.

Table 9-5. Industries targeted by region (percent indicating industry at top 5 priority)

Industry	West	Midwest	South	Northeast
Accommodation and food service	14%	7%	9%	10%
Manufacturing - advanced	35%	49%	43%	55%
Manufacturing - alternative energy	50%	40%	36%	42%
Manufacturing - traditional	20%	49%	41%	26%
Retail	30%	15%	21%	12%
Tourism	22%	13%	14%	15%

In the last survey, Midwestern organizations were found to spend the most of any region on websites. This time around, Northeastern organizations prioritize websites the most, allocating 21% of their total marketing budget on average to websites when each of the other regions allocated only a 16% average budget share.

Given the presence of social media internet companies in both the northeast and the west, one might expect that social media usage would be highest among EDOs in those areas. Interestingly, that was not the case. Midwestern organizations were the most likely to have Facebook Pages (78%) and LinkedIn groups for their organizations (65%), while Southern organizations were most likely to have Twitter accounts (62%). Northeastern organizations were most likely to have blogs.

Table 9-6. Does your organization engage in the following social media strategies?

Social Media Platform	Midwest	Northeast	South	West
Facebook Page (for my organization)	78%	74%	75%	67%
Twitter account	54%	55%	62%	53%
LinkedIn group (for my organization)	65%	57%	56%	51%
Blog	32%	37%	26%	29%

Benchmarking

10

"Would you tell me, please, which way I ought to go from here?"
"That depends a good deal on where you want to get to," said the Cat.
"I don't much care where--" said Alice.
"Then it doesn't matter which way you go," said the Cat.
                    - Charles Lutwidge Dodgson, *Alice in Wonderland*

Jobs are still the most often used criteria to benchmark an organization's success by a large margin. The recession has put an even greater pressure on EDOs and public officials to spur job creation, even as the creation of jobs has become increasingly difficult.

Table 10-1. Criteria for benchmarking the success of an EDO (percent indicating measure as one of five most important criteria)

Benchmarking Criterion	% of ED pros Rating Criterion as Important
Jobs created	83%
Capital investment	68%
Announced projects	60%
Increased revenue and/or sales tax to government	46%
Businesses started	44%
Increased wages and benefits	25%
Growth of economic output	25%
Decreased building vacancies and new real estate development	24%
Diversity of industry	19%
Workforce skills level increase	13%
New quality of life/place amenities	12%
We do not benchmark our organization's overall performance	9%
Improvement of distressed neighborhoods	8%

Job Creation

Job creation is the number one benchmark for EDOs. It far outpaces the runner up and has continued to keep its position in first place. However, while unemployment is high and the number of new jobs created is slow in the economic recovery, significant job creation will remain a challenge to attain. It is made even more difficult because the top three industry targets of EDOs are manufacturing, a sector that has lost 20% of its jobs from 2004 to 2010.[30]

This is not a reflection of manufacturing productivity, as it has continued to grow. But it is growing through efficiencies and technology so that more manufacturing output is being created with less people. EDOs' priorities of job creation and targeting manufacturing are at odds with each other as employment trends show that manufacturing jobs continue to decline.

EDOs which are focused on job creation should also consider targeting the industry sectors which are growing jobs such as education, health care, social assistance, arts, entertainment, and professional and business services. Those EDOs focused on manufacturing and job creation should identify the specific sectors of manufacturing that are creating jobs.

There is not as much consensus among EDOs as to how to benchmark their marketing efforts. When we asked EDOs how they benchmark their marketing back in 2007, the top write-in option for the "other" selection was that that they did not benchmark their marketing programs at all. We made that its own option this time around, and unfortunately, but perhaps not surprisingly, the top rated benchmarking strategy was "no formal benchmarking", shared by 20% of EDOs. An essential part of improving performance is measuring performance, and one in five EDOs are missing this key step of successful marketing. This finding dovetails with another recent survey by Development Counsellors International (DCI), which found that the greatest challenge economic development marketers faced was in measuring their impact, even greater than challenges related to funding and staffing.[31] The increasing availability of performance measurement and tracking tools at little to no cost will hopefully help reduce this challenge in the future, but for now many EDOs are simply at a loss.

Table 10-2. Criteria for benchmarking the success of an EDO's marketing efforts (percent rating measure as most important)

Benchmarking Criterion	% of ED pros Rating Criterion as Important
No formal benchmarking	20%
Company locations	19%
Leads generated	17%
Awareness/recall of your organization	11%
Change of perception about community	8%
Site visits	6%
Internet/website traffic	5%
Number of businesses contacted	3%
RFPs sent to you	2%
Other	2%
Media coverage/mentions	2%
Phone calls or e-mails to your organization	2%
Proposals given	2%

Of the eleven options, excluding "no benchmarking" or "other", seven are directly related to action taken by a business that gives an EDO the opportunity to sell their community as a location for investment. For example, leads generated and site visits are measurable impacts in the decision funnel toward a potential investment showing direct interest from a business. However three of the eleven may not lead a business to invest at all. Awareness of an organization, change of perception, and media coverage are awareness touch points with businesses that do not mean they will invest. It is important for EDOs to recognize that the awareness of your organization (3rd place) and change of perception about your community (4th place) may occur, but that they will have very little value to the EDO if those changes don't cause the business to invest. Just knowing you exist is not enough because it's reasonable for businesses to be aware that there are EDOs nearly everywhere they might locate.

Jonathan Bittner from the Anchorage Economic Development

Corporation provides some suggestion. "The new model in our office is: if you can't track it, don't do it", he says. "With e-newsletters we can see who opens it, which links they click on, how long they stay on the article, if they forward it to someone else, etc. Same goes for our website content. The only thing I can measure when I send out a print piece is what time it's picked up by the postal service and how much it costs me to send it out."[32]

The failure of many EDOs to benchmark their marketing hints at larger uncertainties within EDO marketing programs in general. "Opportunities to learn how to be better at marketing economic development appear to be lacking," one respondent wrote. "If they aren't lacking, I'm not easily learning about them." When those who are eager to learn are having difficulty finding relevant training sources, it suggests that the existing training programs could ironically benefit from better self-marketing.

Conclusions

11

"You've got to be very careful if you don't know where you're going, because you might not get there."

– Yogi Berra

The responses we received from ED pros help elucidate not only the current state of economic development marketing, but also where it is headed. A recap of what we have learned:

- Emerging from the economic downturn, EDOs are displaying a newfound sense of optimism about the effectiveness of most economic development marketing practices, and this optimism extends to how they feel about their own efforts.
- ED pros and site selectors agree that websites are the most effective source of communication for economic development. The EDO's website is the first point of contact that site selectors have with an organization, and in the first two phases of site selection, site selectors were considerably more likely to visit an EDO website than to contact an EDO. When marketing effectiveness is compared to budget allotments, websites are still shown to be extremely cost effective compared to traditional strategies.
- ED pros change their behaviors slowly. For the first book, we assumed that the release of the information about the misalignment of resources with marketing effectiveness would lead to a realignment where higher-performing marketing strategies would receive the highest budgets. However, this book shows that the inertia is strong for funding underperforming marketing strategies with significant budget resources. Many of the same large-budget and low-effectiveness strategies from the first survey are the same as the current survey. This resistance of EDOs to change in the face of strong evidence show-

ing what works is an opportunity for nimble EDOs that are open to new and effective marketing.

- Online advertising is growing in importance and perceived value within economic development. It also aligns well with quantifiable benchmarking, as online advertising continues to be one of the most easily measurable forms of marketing.

- Marketing strategies that involve personal contact, such as trade shows and out-of-town meetings, are receiving a greater share of EDO budgets at the expense of strategies that involve printed materials, such as print advertising, direct mail, and brochures. Ninety-seven percent of site selectors reported personally contacting an economic development organization during the process of site selection, which once again shows the value of expert economic development staff in the business site location process.

- EDOs with larger service areas and consequently larger budgets were able to spend a greater share of their overall budget on marketing.

- Social media is growing in importance within the economic development space, in part because it does not need a large budget in order to have an impact. ED pros working with site selectors need to be aware that site selectors are more actively using Linkedin and blogs than they are. EDOs have some catching up to do if they want to reach site selectors where their eyeballs are already pointing.

- EDOs and site selectors are not well aligned across many industries that each are targeting. Those EDOs working with site selection consultants and corporate real estate professionals need to be aware of which industries site selectors are working with and if those industries align with EDO industry targets. The industry site selectors served more than any other was corporate headquarters, yet this was targeted by only 18% of ED pros. The targeting of traditional manufacturing by EDOs actually lines up with the servicing needs of site selectors, which is very encouraging for skeptics who may have thought this sector was on its deathbed. The newer manufacturing subsectors are receiving disproportionately more attention from EDOs than site selectors, but that should not be viewed as wasted attention as these subsectors are expected to experience rapid growth in the near future.

- EDOs are doing more to increase the value of their websites than we had found in our previous study. Today, 98% of EDOs use a website analytics service to track visitors to their websites, up from 71% in 2007. EDOs are also making good on their past pledges to make their website features more interactive for geographic information systems (GIS), sites and buildings, demographics and labor force, and businesses. The profession is very close to a landscape in which the majority of EDO websites will be interactive.

- Effective marketers were a lot more likely to update their website frequently, and they were more likely to have website features like GIS tools for site selection analysis.

- Where an EDO comes from and how it is structured strongly influences its marketing tendencies. Economic development corporations devoted more staff time to marketing than government agencies, though government agencies somehow reported significantly more activity on Twitter and Facebook. Large, urban EDOs in the Northeast were more likely to target advanced manufacturing, whereas rural EDOs in the Midwest and South focused more on traditional manufacturing. Alternative energy was made a higher priority in the West, along with retail and tourism. Urban EDOs were more likely to use each of the social media platforms, but interestingly the activity was higher in the South and Midwest than in the usual tech strongholds of the Northeast and the West. Northeastern organizations gave the highest budget share of any region to websites, taking the crown owned by the Midwest in our last survey.

- EDOs most often benchmark their marketing efforts by the number of leads they generate. However, 20% of EDOs do not benchmark their marketing at all. EDOs that want to be able to prove their value, especially when it comes to justifying funding, should think long and hard about how they can measure their success and remain accountable.

One school of thought about marketing is that you market what you have. You might want your product, which in the case of ED pros is a community, to be better, but you market what you have. Another school of thought is that the best marketing is making the product better. Sales people at companies frequently blame the product people for not making a product that is so good it sells itself. Of course, if it was so good it sold itself, that wouldn't be selling. That's order taking.

ED pros are in a similar situation, and we cannot afford to be ideological in choosing to either market what we have or making it better so that it sells itself. We must do both.

Although I hear some ED pros say that a community must get "its house in order" before marketing it, that position is too detached from the urgency of most communities' economic situations. Unless your community can wait for economic investment, you have an obligation to market what you have now. And you have to improve your community along the way. These two initiatives are a complement to each other and are not in conflict.

A business can't invest in a community it doesn't know about, or if the business doesn't know how it will become more successful by being in a particular location. However, the ways that businesses are discovering the communities that best match their business needs are evolving, and so are the ways that communities are communicating their advantages.[33] Together, they are disrupting traditional ideas of economic development marketing.

This book is designed to help you become a more effective marketer, but it is not an instruction manual to teach you how to do economic development marketing. *You* are the marketing solution you've been waiting for.

Case Studies

12

While an examination of the trends in economic development marketing from a high perch can be very illuminating, it is also valuable to look at the examples of truly innovative people and organizations and their marketing approaches. So we invited expert economic development colleagues to share some of their favorite examples of work they were involved with to give insight into how they effectively and innovatively marketed communities. These individuals have been kind enough to share their stories so that others can learn from their best practices. These stories cover a variety of different strategies with varying goals.

Traditional business retention and expansion (BRE) programs often involve EDO staff meeting individually with businesses, going through a series of interview questions, and identifying how the EDO can help assist the business. The effectiveness of this model is further limited in challenging economic times. Rapidly unpredictable changes, as well as the scale of the difficulties businesses are facing, are outside of the problem set that EDOs can usually address. While local governments may be able to make a zoning change or façade improvement grant, small businesses are dealing with problems like covering the next payroll, and are unlikely to share these profound anxieties in a BRE interview with strangers. However, in Maricopa they've brought a BRE process to businesses that makes those companies more money.

Enhancing Traditional Business Retention and Expansion Models using Web and Digital Media

- Danielle Casey, Assistant City Manager, City of Maricopa

A highly entrepreneurial community, the City of Maricopa has seen the launch of a high number of new, home-based businesses and independent retail shops following explosive residential growth – from only 1,500 residents in 2000 to nearly 47,000 in 2010.

Raising awareness of local business offerings has been a challenge, with many Maricopa residents working in neighboring metro locations. The City's economic development team was utilizing a traditional business retention and expansion model, with tools such as a visitation program, market research assistance, advocacy, and training programs to support local companies. For communities with limited staffing resources, however, these traditional models do not always produce the biggest bang for the buck. We found it challenging to even get on the calendars of local businesses to conduct retention visits, and for good reason – these are small business owners trying to make a living, they need to work and not sit in meetings with local officials.

After significant brainstorming, the City team found a way to provide assistance to businesses in a way that created measurable value while establishing a platform for holding a relaxed and meaningful dialogue with local owners. Using existing resources only – a media specialist with a camera and editing software, a department director not afraid to be on air, and a public information officer skilled in social media – the team created an opportunity for the first 12 responding local businesses to be interviewed, videotaped, and featured on the City's government channel, each on a separate day from December 13-24, as a holiday shopping initiative: "The 12 Days of Holiday Shopping." "The response by the business community was overwhelming – not only did we fill all 12 spots within about two days, we had nearly 20 businesses already on a waiting list to participate in the permanent program," says Ruben Garcia, City Media Specialist.

Flyer for Maricopa's Business Beat program

Due to popularity, the holiday program evolved immediately into the regular TV production "Business Beat." Local businesses (up to four each month) are interviewed, videotaped, and featured on the City's government access channel throughout a given month. All of this is provided free of charge to local businesses. In addition to airing the spots on the City's channel, Maricopa20, interviews continue to be available online via Maricopa20's YouTube channel, youtube.com/MyMaricopa20, and by syndication via social media outlets. Finally, the City developed web and social media tips as a resource to featured businesses to help them maximize the marketing impact of their videos. "We have been tweeting and Facebooking like crazy, and reminding residents through press releases and newsletters to check out the spots and learn more about their local shopping and service offerings," notes LaTricia Woods, City Public Information Officer. The partnership of the local Chamber of Commerce, along with utilization of other City resources such as a weekly electronic newsletter and bi-monthly print publication, helped spread the word to residents. "The Economic Development Department in our fair city is being really proactive in supporting local businesses and I am very thankful! I can't say enough about how professional the folks from the Economic Development Department and Maricopa20 TV are," exclaimed Brad Bolt, owner of All Aspects Window Cleaning.

Key Program Elements:

- Local businesses license is required
- All participants are required to complete a survey one month following participation to determine where they heard about the program, their impression of its quality, whether they received referrals as a result, and how they utilized the video as a marketing tool
- City conducts 2-4 tapings and airings per month, airs programming on live TV, the City website and YouTube
- City provides social media utilization training to businesses as needed and promotes the videos via all marketing and social media channels

In its first year, the City of Maricopa produced and aired a total of 28 local business features. All participants responded that they would recommend the program to other businesses, and 53% cited direct referral business generated as a result of participation. Fifty percent of participants embedded the videos directly into their own websites, and 69% utilized social media to spread the word. "I believe great marketing is all about keeping your name out there. I recommend this free resource to every business in our community," says Minerva Hendrix, a local Maricopa business owner. It has now become a successful cornerstone of the community's business retention and expansion program.

To learn more about the City's Business Beat program, visit http://businessbeat.maricopa-az.gov. For all of the featured business spots, visit the City's YouTube page at www.youtube.com/MyMaricopa20.

> Economic development's origins are deeply rooted in business attraction. But today businesses are selecting communities for the talent of their labor force, so now EDOs are recruiting talented professionals as a precursor to attracting business investment. As former Hewlett Packard CEO Carly Fiorina said to a conference of governors, "Keep your tax incentives and highway interchanges, we will go where the highly skilled people are."

Got Talent? The Research Triangle Region Unveils Talent Attraction Campaign

- Julie Curtin, Partner/Executive Vice President,
Development Counsellors International (DCI)
and
Erin Bodine, Talent Attraction Director,
Development Counsellors International (DCI)

In 2010, the Research Triangle Region of North Carolina was at an exciting crossroads, continuing to lead the country on nearly every measure of economic success. But as the global competition for the world's best and brightest heated up, the community's business leaders recognized that the Triangle needed to continue to cultivate and replenish its most important asset – people – in order for the region to flourish in the decades to come.

The region was projected to grow by more than 700,000 people - or 30 percent - by 2030. As the lead economic development organization for greater Raleigh, N.C., Wake County Economic Development (WCED) wanted to ensure that the Triangle was targeting and attracting workers with the right skills – those that were a match for the region's most needed positions in its top industry clusters, including jobs where technology and other fields, such as healthcare and life sciences, were converging so fast that training and supply for these positions had not yet caught up with demand in their region.

Wake County Economic Development also sought to assist the business community - which lacked a single place to send prospective job candidates for information about the region – by creating a website that would serve as a one-stop-shop and tool for both HR managers and skilled professionals outside the area to get information about the Triangle's incredible quality of place advantages and lifestyle assets.

As part of a five-year plan focused on attracting skilled workers from around the world for the region's thriving target industries, the Wake County Economic Development team engaged DCI in January 2011 to develop and implement a talent attraction marketing campaign to help position the Triangle as one of the best destinations in the world for talented professionals and create a web portal that would advertise and combine all of the region's resources and things to do.

Because the talent attraction initiative would be a regional effort, combining the three cities of Raleigh, Chapel Hill and Durham, along with the 13 different counties that make up the Research Triangle region, the campaign would need to have a brand and concept that the entire area could rally around – a difficult task, since each city had its own personality and key messages in place already. To do this, DCI assisted WCED in conducting one-on-one interviews with more than 40 regional business leaders and professionals, along with a perception survey of more than 450 skilled workers in the Triangle, which helped determine the region's strengths and weaknesses, uncover perceptions of the region, and reveal qualities and assets that were truly unique to the greater Triangle.

Using the results of the qualitative interviews and survey as the foundation for a regional brand and further recommendations, DCI created a new consumer-focused concept centered on the idea that the Triangle could really own the word "smart." DCI also then developed an extensive talent attraction marketing blueprint that outlined in detail key tactics to bring the initiative and brand to life, by educating and engaging local stakeholders such as the business community, and share the region's opportunity messages with talented workers outside the Triangle. This integrated marketing communications plan included more than a dozen recommendations and a timeline for the talent attraction campaign in the Triangle.

From there, DCI helped the region flesh out the new talent attraction brand, logo and tagline – Work in the Triangle, Smarter from Any Angle - that captured the Triangle's value proposition for skilled professionals. DCI's research indicated that the Triangle truly was a smart choice for talented workers, because people could have a smart career in a growing industry; a smart lifestyle, because they could live outdoors year-round and pay comparatively less for housing than in many other major metro areas; and be in a region with smart people doing smart things with the three major research universities in such close proximity.

DCI also partnered with WCED to help the organization launch an ambassador program - once again capitalizing on the smart theme, calling the ambassadors Triangle Smarty Pants – to engage local target audiences in the campaign and help skilled professionals outside the region connect with those already working in the triangle. An initial group of 30 ambassadors from the region were deployed to spread the positive news about the Triangle via personal and social media interactions, using the hashtag #workinthetriangle. These ambassadors immediately began engaging their vast networks on a regular basis, using #workinthetriangle to share all of the great things going on in their area with other professionals across the country and around the world.

On May 9, 2012, WCED hosted a 250-attendee launch event featuring Forbes writer and noted demographer Joel Kotkin, a key recommendation from DCI's marketing plan, to unveil the campaign locally among target audiences. This was a critical part of the campaign, since it was the first time the organization was seeking the larger community's buy-in and assistance. Using a social media strategy for the event developed by DCI, the Triangle gained 100 new Twitter followers the day of the launch. A few months later, WCED held its first target market event and kicked off the campaign externally at the BIO Career Fair as one of only two communities exhibiting at the job fair with its new trade show booth. Wake County Economic Development met more than 400 biotech professionals there, gathering hundreds of resumes and engaging with them via social media through a plan developed and executed with DCI.

Advertisement for BIO International conference program

WCED also revealed its new talent attraction website portal, www. WorkintheTriangle.com, including a microsite for the campaign's ambassadors. DCI oversaw the development of content, design, and production of this outlet along with several marketing collateral pieces, including brochures, trade show booths, ads and giveaways. The website had 1,400 unique visitors the first month of the campaign and is averaging about 2,000 monthly visitors to date. DCI also helped Wake County Economic Development initiate an aggressive media relations campaign to share the key messages of the campaign with a broader national audience via editorial placement, including a story placed on FOX & Friends featuring Triangle company Bandwidth.com's 30 job openings, and a 6-minute podcast on the influential life sciences trade outlet *The Burrill Report* prior to BIO.

As with all economic development organizations, WCED also needed to demonstrate the value of its work to its investors, regional partners, and the business community. Through the Work in the Triangle, Smarter from Any Angle campaign, it has done just that, solidifying partnerships with its economic development organizations by engaging them in the process and initiative, and receiving incredibly positive responses to the campaign from company leaders. Interest in participating in the campaign from local corporations was also overwhelming. Companies saw the website as a valuable resource in their recruiting and retention efforts, and the Work in the Triangle campaign helped fill in an important gap, allowing WCED to play a critical role in the community's focus on attracting the right talent.

> EDOs with effective online GIS-based site selection analysis assistance programs can't imagine how they were ever able to do their work before they had these programs in place. Yet too many EDOs are operating without this technology advantage. In Western New York, the ED pros have taken their economic development to the next level with a GIS website that provides high-quality site selection assistance and helps local entrepreneurs grow their companies through business intelligence and market analysis.

Site Selection & the Internet: Buffalo Niagara's Commercial Listing System

- Christopher Finn, Research Manager, Buffalo Niagara Enterprise

A primary objective of Buffalo Niagara Enterprise (BNE) is to assist location consultants or corporate real estate executives during "site selection". Those unfamiliar with the industry often associate this term with real estate; however, the term encompasses a lengthy set of criteria that needs to be supported by a wealth of data. It incorporates tax and incentive data, knowledge of environmental and permitting concerns, demographic and labor market analyses, evaluating utility infrastructure, plus much more. A typical project sends BNE a multi-page request for information (RFI) and our response is a one-inch thick binder of data.

Distributed to select communities, the RFI document allows the site selector to compare regions at the quantitative level, absent marketing campaigns or PR efforts. But how were the communities first chosen? In the internet age, site selectors are performing due diligence online and through their own databases. Communities are now being ruled out, before they knew they were a consideration.

While seemingly intimidating, this preliminary evaluation and elimination process affords an opportunity to EDOs that are willing to invest in providing easy and comprehensive access to information. Present the data these executives are seeking, in their desired format, and a region may get included in the RFI phase.

BNE acknowledges that our website is the front door to our organization. From 1999 to 2009, an enormous effort went into presenting regional data on our website to our target audience, but this was static data. The user was not able to customize what they received, they were only able to access what was posted; and as soon as it was posted, it was out of date. However the technology was not yet available, or affordable, to represent custom and up-to-date data on the region regarding demographics, business, and other key data points. Realizing this data is critical to not only business attraction efforts, but also for the local small business and entrepreneurial community, BNE undertook the initiative to bridge this gap and brought GIS Planning's GIS based site selection analysis information platform to western New York. The program is called the Buffalo Niagara Commercial Listing Service (CLS) and it is available at www.BuffaloNiagaraCLS.com.

Realizing that successful attraction projects resulting from the platform may take time to evolve, a focus was placed on distributing the platform's potential to our local partners. BNE met with business organizations, local chambers, industrial development agencies, and utility partners over the course of a year. This effort provided multiple benefits. First, it allowed these groups to better understand their local business community and even conduct business retention and expansion campaigns. Secondly, it allowed these groups to offer the services of the platform to the companies they worked with directly. Lastly, these groups were able to offer the tools to the public within their respective local communities. Entrepreneurs, grant writers, and even students were provided access to free, custom, and local data. In the past, a grant writer might have settled for 10-year old demographic data and typically for a region much larger than their focus geography. Now they can access current year demographic and industry data for any geography. From county datasets, to municipal data, even to custom drive times or radii searches, the data is truly user-defined. An entrepreneur can now come to Buffalo Niagara CLS, find a piece of commercial real estate, and examine the market immediately surrounding the site as well as the region. They can then analyze the local consumer spending patterns on over 60 segments of commercial products and services, and then examine local competition or supply chains. Gathering this data ten years ago would have been time consuming and expensive for a segment of people who have little time or money to spend. Utilizing the Buffalo Niagara CLS platform, it can be accessed in minutes and for free.

Business report on Buffalo Niagara CLS

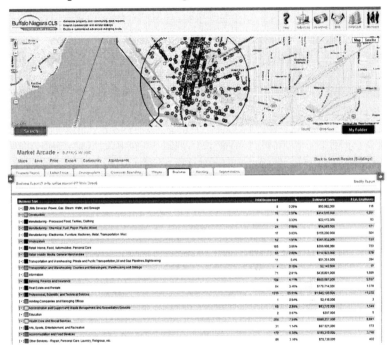

A common question that any EDO or even commercial real estate broker wrestles with is how much information should be given to the public? Specifically, at what point do we cease providing data and force the user to reach out to our group, capturing the opportunity directly? Does offering a limited amount of data entice the user to pick up the phone or does it put them off and force them to seek communities that do offer the data? Having this technology does allow an individual to access the data they sought and then potentially move on unsatisfied, perhaps as the result of misunderstanding the data or not using the website correctly. BNE acknowledges all of these risks, but felt the reward was larger. It's more important to offer the data and potentially lose a project than to not be considered for a project at all. Furthermore, BNE cares above all else that projects come to the region, not that a project comes because of BNE's assistance.

Just as critical as having this data is tracking its use, because justifying a significant investment through its ROI is essential. Current technology on our website not only allows tracking of basic website activity, but EDOs can now also see which companies are looking at their site. While no one will ever get to see what person is looking, knowing what company is looking at your site and they pages they are viewing is a huge advantage for business attraction efforts. The site analytics are just as valuable. For example, BNE can track the number of data reports that have been accessed and properties that have been viewed. BNE can say with confidence that we are bringing value not only to our website and our target audience but the local community as well.

Offering data is not a panacea to win every project. We do not rely on these tools to close projects for us, but instead view them as an opportunity to get us in the door. GIS and data platforms will never replace personal relationships that create attraction opportunities for western New York. We've seen it first hand over the past 13 years: once our region makes a first cut, if we do not win the deal, we win over the site selector. That is the number one way to get Buffalo Niagara involved with its next project. The data platform gives us the opportunity to be in that first cut and the opportunity to create that personal relationship.

> Economic development, like business and friendships, is still about the people. We are in a profession that is relationship-based and people still like to do business with people they know, like, and trust. I've known Kenny McDonald for a long time and he probably racks up more airline miles in a year than most people do in a lifetime. Face-to-face interactions build deeper relationships, one meeting at a time. If you haven't yet logged the miles he has with the results he's produced, you can skip ahead by learning what he's learned.

Lessons from the Road

- Kenny McDonald, Chief Economic Officer, Columbus 2020

Economic development is a profession that requires both the desire and willingness to connect people and develop personal, trusting relationships so that big things can be accomplished in our communities. Relationships are not formed overnight, and many require years to develop and deliver results. Others serendipitously produce results almost immediately, but can only be achieved if you put yourself – and your community – in the arena where growing companies and location advisors live and breathe.

As a regional economic development professional, I have had the opportunity to travel all over the world meeting companies and the various location advisors that help to guide businesses considering expansions and relocations. I've called upon hundreds of location advisors and knocked on a lot of doors, and enjoyed every minute of it. I have been supported by great teams of researchers that have helped me to target specific industry associations, individual companies, and location advisory teams. However, three basic principles guide my efforts.

First, you can't get lucky if you are not in the room. Many times, I have picked up intelligence about a project or met a person that has become critical to connecting to a prospect by attending the reception that I didn't want to go to, sitting in on an information session at a tradeshow, or by casually starting a conversation with someone at an event. You can't be everywhere, but if you are attending something, give it your full attention.

Second, always make one more call. One time in Atlanta at the end of a long day of calling on location advisors, I had on my schedule to meet one more broker from a relatively unknown firm. I had trouble finding the location, but eventually we connected for a brief meeting. Within one month, he had purchased a building in our region, and within six months, hundreds of people were working at that very facility for a client he had led to the location. I recall that experience often and always try to make one more call.

Finally, never have a bad meeting. I have attended many introductory meetings with location advisors and company executives that seemingly went poorly. This is made more uncomfortable if you are with your city's mayor or other public officials, who look at you with a wary eye upon leaving the building. I try to prepare my group for trips by recalling these maxims: What can we learn from the meeting or the event? And, what perceptions do people have about our region or state? Often, I find these the most important meetings of all, as they provide perspective. Companies have many choices, and your community is not always the right fit. It also provides a clear opportunity to, over time, change those perceptions by educating the location advisor or the client about your community. Honest feedback is a blessing, not a curse.

I encourage ED pros and public officials to meet with companies, put themselves in the arena, make one more call and see what happens, and take at least one thing away from each encounter or meeting.

> I was a judge giving awards for innovative economic development marketing when I learned about the "Why Baltimore" campaign. I still refer to it as one of the most innovative initiatives of our profession. It's an interesting combination of guerrilla marketing with a theoretical analysis of the importance of the Creative Class before there was popular understanding of the Creative Class. I continue to imagine the power of commuting into to work and being confronted with the question "Why Baltimore?"

Why Baltimore? Blazing New Trails for Regional Economic and Community Development

- Ioanna T. Morfessis, Ph.D., President and Chief Strategist, IO.INC

The Challenge and Opportunity

In the late 1990s, it was apparent that the availability of talent would soon emerge as a major driver of where companies located, invested, and created jobs. At the same time, and across all sectors of the economy, workers were beginning to demand more for their lives, consequently seeking more from their employers and the communities in which they lived.

For Greater Baltimore, it was equally apparent that the region could ill afford to let demography become its destiny. The community was facing a deficit of young workers, primarily represented by Gen X and Gen Y. Population projections showed an alarming net deficit of 100,000 workers in the 25-44 age group over the next ten years (2000-2010).

Recognizing that this drive for talent and the impending deficit of younger workers would significantly impact the future of the Greater Baltimore region, the Economic Alliance of Greater Baltimore formally initiated its "Branding Greater Baltimore" strategy in 1999. In order to prevent and remediate the looming talent deficit, we knew that our regional economic development strategy had to embrace an entirely new approach and integrate an effective people recruitment and retention strategy. Achieving and sustaining population growth

– especially among the Gen X and Gen Y cohorts - was mission critical for the entire community.

The questions we needed to answer were basic. Could we adequately predict what kind of workforce would be required to meet the demand of current and future employers? What would people want – especially young people - not only from the companies for whom they worked, but also from the communities in which they lived? In 1999 and ten years hence?

To help refine and answer these questions, the Economic Alliance of Greater Baltimore (EAGB) joined with Brain Reserve, a leading consumer trend forecasting company led by Faith Popcorn, and Arthur Andersen's Global Business Location Services, led by Dan Malachuk, to bring an unorthodox approach to our task. Together, we garnered industry, government, education, arts, youth and civic leaders to evaluate the landscape, envision the future and develop a blueprint for sustained economic success in the Greater Baltimore region. The EAGB cast a wide net in selecting project participants to represent the region's socially, economically, and ethnically diverse population.

Together, this group charted new territory for economic development and community branding by fusing traditional business site selection principles with an unprecedented, people-driven approach that clearly differentiated Greater Baltimore from other regions throughout the nation, and perhaps the world.

Ask, Listen, and Act

Partnering with Brain Reserve and Arthur Anderson Global Business Locations, the EAGB convened focus groups in major cities across the U.S. – including Baltimore - to ask Gen X'ers and Gen Y'ers how a region could best attract and retain workers in these generational cohorts. We asked the questions that would tell us what needed to be done across all spectrums of community and society to be one of the most attractive communities for these young people. The result? We learned that the most critical location determinants for Gen X, Y and those in between were:

- Public safety
- Enlightened, innovative companies
- Quality schools
- Convenient public transportation
- Abundant blue and green spaces
- A welcoming community open to newcomers and diversity

The Branding Baltimore Initiative established both an economic development and community improvement agenda for Greater Baltimore. To that end, the following strategies were implemented:

- A marketing strategy designed to retain and attract the best companies for the best talent.
- Internal and external marketing and communications campaigns aimed at retaining and attracting Generation X and Y workers.
- A strategy designed to train and provide a highly skilled workforce to meet the growth and expansion requirements of the business community.
- A product improvement agenda for government and business, carried out principally by the Baltimore Community Foundation and other philanthropic and community organizations.

Why Baltimore?

Through our research, we discovered that one of the most significant drags on Greater Baltimore's image from a youth and young adult perspective was Baltimoreans' own perceptions of their community. It was clear that the EAGB had to aggressively pursue a multi-faceted approach, and the internal communications strategy would first have to improve local perceptions of the region, and also reach youth/young adults with credible and meaningful messages.

As part of the focus group process, the participants were asked: What do you know about Baltimore? What do you like about Baltimore? What do you dislike about Baltimore? What would it take to improve your image and liking of Baltimore?

Based on these responses, the EAGB created the Why Baltimore? Campaign as our initial communications strategy to reaffirm/reinforce all of the positive attributes of the community. For three months, the campaign featured answers to the question "Why Baltimore?" in print ads, on the Internet, and on billboards along Maryland's Interstate highways: "Love them Orioles, hon." "Seafood and crabs." "Baltimore Symphony." "Inner Harbor." "Historic places." "Federal Hill." In each instance, the advertisement was simply the answer without the question.

These messages – simple two and three word phrases citing unique qualities and attributes of the community - titillated the public and local media. After three months of advertising these various phrases, the EAGB then moved into its next phase, simply offering the question, "Why Baltimore?" The ads and billboards made sense to most everyone, and more than 80 cities across the nation took a hard look at the campaign, with many replicating our work. The campaign ignited a sense of pride and positivism that translated into a greater sense of connectivity to the region. One simple question – "Why Baltimore?" – cleverly extrapolated the many reasons that connected citizens to their community, and their answers were in direct relation to what our research suggested: people locate and live in places where they feel a sense of belonging and opportunity.

Over time, "Why Baltimore?" morphed into its next stages: "Be. Be in Baltimore," and ultimately, into the "Believe in Baltimore" campaign.

> ED pros have tried to use multiple media to communicate the value proposition of their community for business investment. Whether it was an advertisement in a newspaper or a public relations placement in a major business magazine, we went through media to deliver information. Now, because of social technology, we are the media.

Think Maryland

- Alissa Sklar,[34] Ph.D. VP, Social Media Services, ROI Research On Investment

Think Maryland, and what comes to mind? Crab cakes? The Baltimore Orioles? The Star Spangled Banner? Think again. The Maryland Department of Business and Economic Development (DBED) is working hard on using social media through their website ChooseMaryland.org to direct attention to their prime mid-Atlantic location, highly educated, diverse workforce, proximity to the nation's capital, and more. DBED effectively spreads strategic messages on how Marylanders live, work, and play. They are such a good example that I can easily use DBED when illustrating to clients of ROI Research on Investment just what is possible in the world of social media.

In 2010, the tech blog Mashable identified DBED as an EDO with innovative use of social media,[35] and their sites are standing the test of time. Their extremely active and relatively mature accounts on Facebook, Twitter, YouTube, Flickr and LinkedIn showcase the way these tools can be used to tell your community's story, seed the search with key terms, engage business clients for retention, promotion and relocation. It makes sense to begin with YouTube, since ChooseMaryland.org features the video sharing site prominently in a widget placed front and center on their landing page. Viewers are invited to click on their video "The Truth About Maryland" to see a quick overview of statistics, facts, and figures about the state. The frequently updated MarylandBiz channel (active since 2009) features over 178 videos and racks up an impressive total view count nearing 73,000. Some of these videos are announcements, others are company profiles, and some are part of their innovative "Why Maryland" series, in which individual business owners explain why the state is the right place for their business.

The DBED's official Twitter feed (@MDBiz) is a mature account, with over 6,000 followers and more than 4,200 Tweets. Posts average several per day and are mostly in the form of news announcements, links to reports, articles, and new video uploads to the YouTube site. The account makes strong use of hashtags and keywords, but doesn't generally engage with followers or others in the Twittersphere.

DBED has a large Flickr photostream. This is updated sporadically, based on the traditional events that occasion such photos: trade shows, press conferences, facility tours, business forums, etc. While most images are typical of corporate and administrative events (groups of smiling people posed in front of banners), many do have descriptive captions (critical for SEO, and too often overlooked with photo uploads). Mentions of regional business featured in images and videos are a critical way to increase loyalty and retention, and they play directly into the share-ability of social media elements.

The images on DBED's Pinterest account are particularly engaging, which makes perfect sense. Given the visual bias of this particular social media tool, it's critical that images used to represent these pages capture attention and recommend themselves for repinning by followers. One of their four boards highlights their Land of Opportunity poster series (featuring regional business owners), others show images of local products, businesses, and landscapes, and most have very brief descriptions. Not too surprisingly (given that Pinterest is a relative newcomer on the social media scene), this is a young account, and it isn't linked to ChooseMaryland.org, though this may well be the direction they are moving as more images are added and followers sought.

DBED has an excellent, thorough company page on LinkedIn with 515 followers. The organization description offers a gold standard for other EDOs seeking an example of keyword optimization and concise, readable text. DBED also has an active group on LinkedIn with respectable membership (656 people). It maintains and promotes its

Wikipedia page, and a note on the site flags it for neutrality questions.

DBED succeeds in making a credible social media splash where too many other EDOs are entirely absent or generally ineffective. They inject color into the conversation, cut through the clutter on-line, and in working effectively for both retention and investment attraction, they are potentially making a difference where it really counts – in their bottom line.

It would be nice to think that there is a marketing silver bullet and that if we did just one thing right, everything would work. The reality is that a holistic approach is more typically required. However, a scatter-shot approach will only lead to failure. As Larry Weber, author of Marketing to the Social Web, says, "For the past 10 years, corporations have been trained that they should use all the different media…but the Internet is becoming the umbrella." In southwestern Indiana, they strategically used the umbrella of the Internet and offline marketing to deliver a holistic initiative.

Holistic Marketing

- Jim Walton, CEO, Brand Acceleration, Inc.

Marketing a city, county, or region presents special challenges, and marketing Warrick County, Indiana was no different. When Brand Acceleration was selected to handle the county's marketing communications and public relations, the decision was made to take a much more holistic approach.

Rather than trying one tactic at a time, hoping for miracles, or the silver bullet approach, the team took a hard look at the identified industries, matched them to target audiences, and then crafted a broad plan to grow awareness.

With outstanding interstate highway connections and the benefits of the Ohio River, Warrick County, Indiana was in a great position for growth, providing a lifestyle and business benefits that are hard to beat. Our challenge was to develop a well-thought-out strategy and a series of tactics that visually and verbally communicated these benefits to prospective and existing businesses, residents, and visitors.

After working with the county to produce a new name (Success Warrick County), logo, and slogan, we launched two new web sites, one for economic development and one for the tourism market. Once the web sites were in place, a very powerful outreach initiative was launched. A series of carefully crafted and highly programmed e-mailers were distributed directly to site selection consultants, real estate professionals, and c-suite executives in an effort to drive these desirable audiences to the new web site. Not surprisingly, the web traffic spiked dramatically, exactly as expected. Additionally, we produced an entire package of brochures in English and Japanese, stationery items, and public relations tactics.

Another very significant part of the community's marketing effort was focused on their new health and wellness district named Warrick Wellness Trail. A ground-up project was developed out of 1,400 acres of farm land. The goal was to position the county as a regional healthcare destination, serving a region of over one million residents in several states. As of this writing, the area is experiencing very significant growth, including multiple hospitals, clinics, medical practices, retirement facilities, and health-related retail. Overall, this project has been a big plus for the county, making it even more attractive for traditional attraction and retention projects.

In the summer of 2012, a major PGA golf tournament was held in Warrick County, attracting thousands of visitors. Pulling out all the stops, the economic development organization partnered with local groups to staff parking areas and to capitalize on the opportunity to tell its story. Dressed in branded attire, volunteers handed each visitor a card featuring the area's top selling points. Plus, a promotional kiosk was placed in the airport, featuring the area sales pitch and a QR code. During the days of the golf tournament, web traffic via mobile devices skyrocketed, proving that the grassroots effort had succeeded.

In summary, what we anticipated and found was that our holistic approach was right on. We effectively crafted a message strategy and rolled it out through multiple platforms: web sites, e-mail marketing, naming, social media, signs, and public relations.

> Although economic development may have a mythology of heroic ED pros making deals in steak houses over multiple cocktails, the future superman of the profession is the Big Data analyst. As research has proved, gut-feelings are not only unreliable, they can be disastrous. Intuition is being replaced with solid research utilizing big data analysis, made possible through the explosion of data and computing power. The only economic development that can succeed in the future will be smart economic development.

Predictive Analytics as an Existing Business Services Early Warning System

- Dean Whittaker, Founder and CEO, Whittaker Associates

Predictive analytics is a powerful tool to dramatically improve target marketing by focusing resources on those companies most likely to respond to the marketing message of economic development organizations.

Columbus2020 was eager to get their business retention and expansion efforts underway, so they contracted with Whittaker Associates, Inc. to design and implement an Existing Business Early Warning System (EWS). The challenge was to identify and prioritize the top 300 companies (out of 120,000 businesses) within their ten-county region that would benefit most from their existing business services.

To address this need we used our predictive analytics system. Predictive analytics encompasses a variety of statistical techniques from modeling, machine learning, data mining, and game theory that analyze current and historical facts to make predictions about future events. Whittaker Associates, Inc., applies predictive analytics to predict corporate behavior. Specifically, they use it to help answer the question, "What companies are likely to expand, relocate, or consolidate their operations in the near future?"

The predictive analytics system ranked companies within the Chamber's multi-county region as to the firm's potential to expand, consolidate, or close operations. The model monitors internal and external changes taking place within each company that would impact their operations such as changes in leadership, ownership, sales, and employment. Using our proprietary algorithm, a matrix of events was created to categorize the firms as to the probability they would expand, consolidate, or close.

The early warning system provides business intelligence to the economic development staff to enable them to more effectively and efficiently provide appropriate services to existing businesses. A web-based business retention system was used to collaborate and share the data among their regional partners, and Columbus2020! internal research staff was trained to maintain the system. As a result, it is known to all of the regional partners which companies are the best candidates for existing business services.

Predictive analytics and "Big Data" are dramatically changing the way in which marketing is done. With the large amount of information available about any target audience, increasingly accurate predictions can be made as to which audiences are most likely to respond to a marketing message, improving both the effectiveness and the efficiency of marketing efforts.

Appendix A: Characteristics of ED Pros Surveyed

Figure A-1. Respondents by state

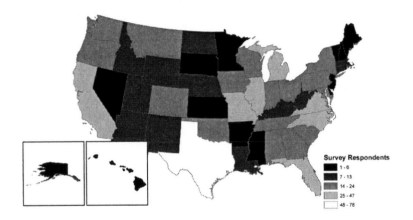

Survey Respondents
- 1 - 6
- 7 - 13
- 14 - 24
- 25 - 47
- 48 - 78

The EDO survey was distributed online to a mailing list of ED pros. It received 767 responses from all 50 states.

Table A-1. State and regional association members represented

Arizona Association for Economic Development
Arkansas Economic Developers
California Association for Local Economic Development
California Redevelopment Association
Connecticut Economic Development Association
Economic Developers of North Dakota
Economic Development Association of Alabama
Economic Development Association of Minnesota
Economic Development Association of New Jersey
Economic Development Council of Colorado
Economic Development Council of Maine
Florida Economic Development Council
Georgia Economic Development Association
Illinois Development Council
Indiana Economic Development Association
Kansas Economic Development Alliance
Kentucky Industrial Development Council
Louisiana Industrial Development Executives Association
Maine Real Estate and Development Association
Maryland Economic Development Association
Massachusetts Economic Development Council
Michigan Economic Developers Association
Mid-America Economic Development Council
Mississippi Economic Development Council

Missouri Economic Development Council
Montana Economic Developers Association
Nebraska Economic Developers Association
Nevada Economic Development Association
New Hampshire Economic Developers Association
New York State Economic Development Council
North Carolina Economic Development Association
Northeastern Developers Association
Ohio Development Association
Oklahoma Economic Development Council
Oregon Economic Development Association
Pacific Northwest Economic Development Council
Pennsylvania Economic Development Association
Professional Developers of Iowa
South Carolina Economic Developer's Association
Southern Economic Development Council
Team New England
Tennessee Industrial Development Council
Texas Economic Development Council
Virginia Economic Development Association
Washington Economic Development Association
West Virginia Economic Developers Council
Wisconsin Economic Development Association
Wyoming Economic Development Association

Figure A-2. What is the population of your service area?

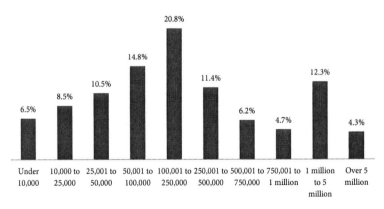

Respondents represented organizations that serviced areas of varying sizes. A large concentration was in the range of 100,000 to 250,000 residents, which constituted a fifth of all responses.

Figure A-3. How would you describe the character of the area served by your organization?

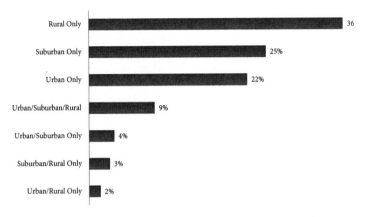

When asked to characterize the area that they served, approximately a third were from rural areas, followed by a fourth from suburban areas, and then a fifth from urban areas.

Figure A-4. What is the structure of your organization?

Government organizations (36% of respondents) and economic development corporations (33%) stood out as the most represented groups in our survey, followed by chambers of commerce (10%) and public-private partnerships (6%). Given that most EDOs are governmental or EDCs, we decided to compare their responses directly.

Figure A-5. My position in the organization

77% of respondents were managers or executives in their organizations.

Figure A-6. My age

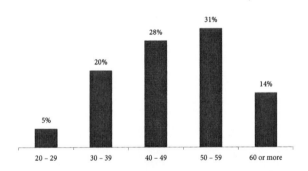

Given the dominant representation of senior-level professionals in the survey, it is not surprising that the majority of the respondents (73%) were over 40 years of age. The over 60 cohort had greater representation (14%) than the below 30 cohort (5%).

Table A-2. What national and international associations are you or your organization a member of? (Top ten associations listed)

Association	% of Respondents Claiming Membership
International Economic Development Council	75%
International Council of Shopping Centers	25%
CoreNet Global	19%
Economic Development Institute	14%
American Planning Association	14%
Council for Community and Economic Research	13%
Urban Land Institute	13%
American Chamber of Commerce Executives	12%
Industrial Asset Management Council	12%
National Development Council	12%

75% of respondents indicated affiliation with the International Economic Development Council, by far the most represented organization. The International Council of Shopping Centers and CoreNet Global were second and third most represented, respectively.

Appendix B: Characteristics of Site Selectors

A survey was distributed online to a mailing list of site selection consultants and corporate real estate professionals. It received 124 responses. This survey is a complement to the economic developer survey, and was significantly shorter.

Table B-1. Companies participating in site selector survey

Adidas Group	Fortum Power and Heat AB	NAI Capital Commercial
Aetna Inc.	Galaxy Organization, The	NetApp
Allen Economic Development Group	Garner Economics	Nokia Siemens Networks
AngelouEconomics	General Motors Corp.	PepsiCo
AOS Studley GmbH	Geyer	Pont Group, The
Atlas Insight	Greenfield Development Company	Procter & Gamble Asia Pte Ltd
Austin Consulting	Grubb & Ellis	PropertyCalc.com
Autodesk	GSP Consulting Corp.	Real Estate Research Consultants
Bain & Company	GVA Grimley	Realvest Partners
Bank of America	Hanesbrands Inc	Redevelopment Resources
CA Commercial Realty Partners	Harrington Consulting Group	Rubin Advisors
Canup & Associates	Have Site Will Travel	ServiceMaster Co, The
Cassidy Turley	Hitachi Data Systems	Sherwin-Williams Co.
CB Richard Ellis	Honeywell Limited	Sitar/ONCOR International
CGR Management Consultants	Humana Inc.	Sodexo Canada
Cisco Systems	IAG New Zealand Ltd	Stanley Black & Decker
CLW Real Estate Services Group	Insight Research Corp.	Steelcase Inc.
Colliers International	Intel Corp.	Stewart Lawrence Group
Computer Associates Intl. Inc.	International Paper Company	Stream Global Services
Continental AG	JEO Consulting Group	SunTrust Bank
Corporate Realty Group	Jones Lang LaSalle	SZD Whiteboard
CorroLuna	KeyBank	TD Bank
CRESA Partners	Kraft Foods Inc.	TIP Strategies
CWS Consulting Group LLC	Lundy Group, The	UGL Equis Corp.
Danaher	Madison Equities	United States Cellular Corporation
Dickinson Consulting Group	Manhattan Centerstone	UnitedHealth Group
Dolby Laboratories Inc.	Marubeni America Corporation	UPC Broadband
eBay	McCallum Sweeney Consulting	Vatterott Educational Centers
EMC International SARL	McCarthy Consulting	Vercitas Group, The
Equis Corporation	McKesson Corporation	Walker Companies, The
Express Scripts Inc.	McShane Construction Co.	Waste Management Inc
ExxonMobil	Mike Barnes Group	Wells Fargo Bank
Fifth Third Bank	Mohr Partners	Zappile Group, The

Figure B-1. What is the area served by your organization?

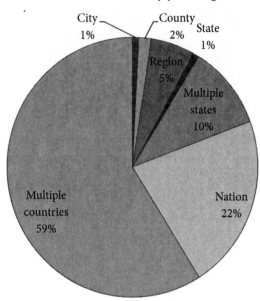

59% of site selectors surveyed served businesses in multiple countries, while an additional 22% served businesses nationwide.

Figure B-2. What are the geographic characteristics of the areas served by your organization?

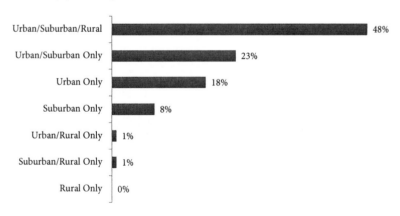

Site selector respondents were more urban and less rural in orientation than the ED Pro respondents. No site selector respondents represented solely rural areas, which was the most common response for ED Pros.

Figure B-3. My role in site selection

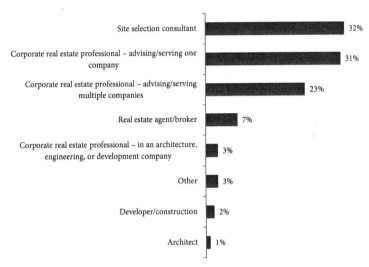

56% of respondents were corporate real estate professionals of one capacity or another, while 32% were site selection consultants.

Figure B-4. My position in the organization

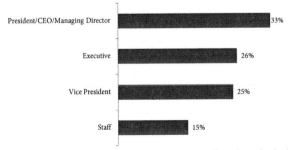

85% of site selector respondents were senior level, a slightly higher share than for the ED Pro respondents.

Appendix C: Additional Charts and Tables

Figure C-1. Total annual ad revenue for site location magazines, 2002-2010

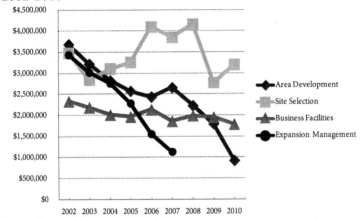

Source: Inquiry Management Systems

Table C-1. Budget change from 2009 to 2010

General Activity	Budget Cut	Budget Increase
Marketing	48%	20%
Business Attraction (outside service area)	37%	12%
Business Expansion (local only)	20%	18%
Business Retention (local only)	19%	21%
Research	19%	8%
Entrepreneurship	17%	19%
Site Selection Assistance	16%	10%
Redevelopment	15%	12%
Real Estate Development	15%	13%
Small Business Development/Support	14%	16%
Job training	14%	10%
Workforce Development	13%	15%
Loan fund	11%	9%
Public Policy	10%	10%
Microenterprise program	9%	4%

Figure C-2. Online advertising's share of total adspend projected, 2010-2014

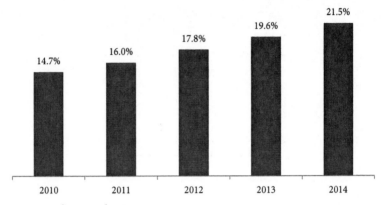

Source: ZenithOptimedia, June 2012

Figure C-3. Advertising revenue market share by media in 2011 (in billions)

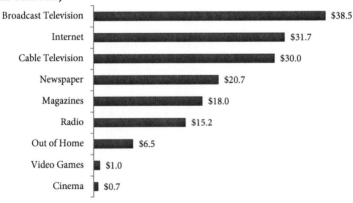

Source: PricewaterhouseCoopers/Interactive Advertising Bureau

Table C-2. Industries serviced most by site selectors

Industry	Targeted by EDOs	Served by Site Selectors
Corporate headquarters	18%	44%
Manufacturing - traditional	36%	36%
Distribution/wholesale trade	30%	36%
Call centers	9%	33%
Finance/insurance	9%	32%
Business services	17%	30%
Information technology/high-technology	29%	27%
Manufacturing - advanced	44%	24%
Research and development	12%	23%
Retail	21%	22%

Figure C-4. Prior to personally contacting an economic development organization to let them know you are considering their community, you typically gather information about communities from:

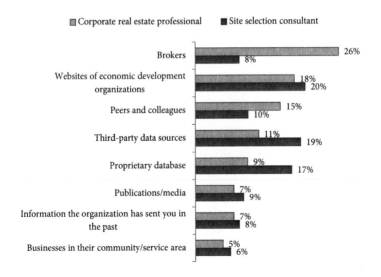

Figure C-5. Value to site selectors of economic development websites that provide site selection analysis technology using geographic information systems (GIS)

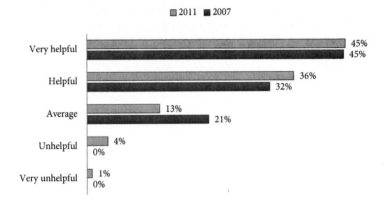

Figure C-6. How often is your website updated?

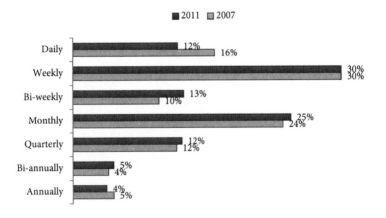

Figure C-7. Percent of ED pros rating social media channel effective (users of the platforms vs. non-users of the platforms)

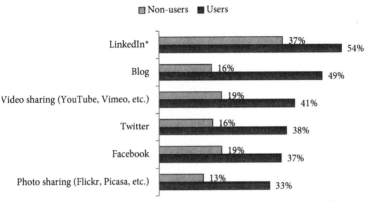

LinkedIn users are here considered to be ED pros that post regularly on discussions

Figure C-8. Percent using social media channels on at least a daily basis

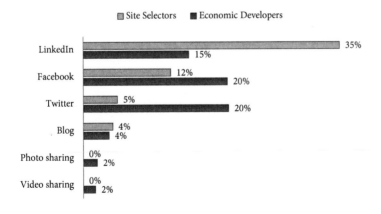

Endnotes

1. "Global Consumers' Trust in 'Earned' Advertising Grows in Importance" (April 10, 2012). Nielsen. Retrieved from http://www.nielsen.com/us/en/insights/press-room/2012/nielsen-global-consumers-trust-in-earned-advertising-grows.html

2. Ubalde, Anatalio & Krueger, Andrew (2011). *Economic Development Online.* (pp. 1).

3. Sanders, Heywood. Space Available: The Realities of Convention Centers as Economic Development Strategy. Washington, DC: Brookings Institution (2005).

4. Center for Exhibition Industry Research (August 29, 2012). Retrieved from http://www.ceir.org

5. Perry, Mark (February 26, 2012). Newspaper Ad Revenues Fall to 60-Yr. Low in 2011 [blog entry]. Retrieved from http://mjperry.blogspot.com/2012/02/newspaper-ad-revenues-fall-to-50-year.html

6. Hof, Robert (January 19, 2012). "Online Ad Revenues to Pass Print in 2012." *Forbes*

7. Indvik, Lauren (August 14, 2012). Google Buys Newspaper Ad to Show Why Newspaper Ads Don't Work [blog entry]. Retrieved from http://mashable.com/2012/08/14/google-print-ad-shows-why-newspaper-ads-dont-work/

8. Szuda, Stephanie (May 23, 2008). "Summit focuses on job struggles in the Illinois Valley", The Times, retrieved from http://mywebtimes.com/archives/ottawa/display.php?id=360365

9. McGuire, Michael. "Collaborative Policy Making and Administration: The Operational Demands of Local Economic Development." Economic Development Quarterly 14, no. 3 (2000): 278-291.

10. Bittner, Jonathan (January 15, 2012). [LinkedIn Post]. Retrieved from http://www.linkedin.com/groupItem?view=&gid=1785140&type=member&item=88674347

11. ZenithOptimedia (June 18, 2012). Global Advertising Continues to Grow Despite Eurozone Fears [blog entry]. Retrieved from http://www.zenithoptimedia.com/zenith/zenithoptimedia-releases-new-ad-forecasts-global-advertising-continues-to-grow-despite-eurozone-fears/.

12. PricewaterhouseCoopers/Interactive Advertising Bureau (April 2012). IAB Internet Advertising Revenue Report [pdf]. Retrieved from http://www.iab.net/media/file/IAB_Internet_Advertising_Revenue_Report_FY_2011.pdf.

13. Invesp Consulting (2008). The State of Online Advertising [pdf]. Retrieved from http://www.invesp.com/docs/invesp-state-of-online-advertising.pdf

14. Southern Economic Development Council 2008 Summer Session (July 10, 2008). Kissimmee, Florida.

15. Sweeney, Mark, personal interview. July 16, 2008.

16. Foote, Deane, personal interview. July 23, 2008.

17. Schjeldahl, Don, personal interview. July 16, 2008.

18. Donovan, Dennis, personal interview. July 16, 2008.

19. Monger, Tim, personal interview. July 16, 2008.

20. Not all companies needing to locate corporate real estate utilize the services of site selectors, as site selection consultants and corporate real estate professionals tend to serve companies that are large employers, are making a large financial investment, or have a high financial value. In particular, small businesses often lack the financial resources to hire a site selector. Industries that include a large share of small businesses may therefore be underrepresented in a site selector survey.

21. Coene, Ted and Bill MacRae (2011). How Executives Use Media During a Site Search [Powerpoint slides]. Retrieved from http://www.businessfacilities.com/pdfs/IDEC_Presentation_

September_2011.pdf

22. The term "site selectors" includes both corporate real estate professionals and site selection consultants.

23. It is very important to note that although a comparison between ED pros and corporate real estate site selectors is provided, the reader of this report should not infer that one of these groups is more correct than the other or that one should follow the tendencies of the other. Instead, it is simply a comparison for use for ED pros that are specifically targeting corporate real estate professionals and site selection consultants. Although there are many thousands of corporate real estate professionals, there are very few boutique site selection consulting companies at all, yet these consultants often get disproportionate attention from ED pros because these companies are often involved in the mega-deal business expansion or relocation projects. We are concerned that, by highlighting them, we may be further supporting the myth that it is site selection consultants that are the key gateway to accessing economic development projects. However, the greatest amount of site selection projects is not being done by site selection consultants. Each year, approximately 750,000 businesses have to make a location decision, and that does not include business relocations (Source: US Small Business Administration). There are tremendous opportunities for EDOs to target this much larger amount of site selection projects being done by businesses themselves.

24. Henderson, Michael (February 23, 2012). [LinkedIn Post] http://www.linkedin.com/groupItem?view=&gid=2919968&type=member&item=96655954,

25. Donovan, Dennis, personal interview. July 16, 2008.

26. Barnes, Nora Ganim and Ava M. Lescault. The 2012 Inc. 500 Social Media Update: Blogging Declines As Newer Tools Rule [PDF]. Retrieved from http://www.umassd.edu/media/umassdartmouth/cmr/studiesandresearch/2011_Inc500.pdf on 8/29/2012.

27. You can read more about Facebook Pages in Chapter 10 of

Economic Development Online by Ubalde & Krueger (2011). If you're looking for an easy way to start adding value to your Facebook Page, you can add demographics and property search to your Facebook Page at http://www.Facebook.com/ZoomProspector.

28. At the time of the survey, Google+ was just emerging as a major social media platform and it was not even included in the survey.

29. Testa, Bill (November 10, 2011). "Nonmetropolitan counties bouncing back." Federal Reserve Bank of Chicago. Retrieved from http://midwest.chicagofedblogs.org/archives/2011/11/nonmetropolitan.html

30. Bureau of Economic Analysis.

31. Curtin, Julie (April 6, 2012). "Place Marketers Say Measurement Is Biggest Challenge." Development Counsellors International. Retrieved from http://www.aboutdci.com/2012/04/place-marketers-say-measurement-is-biggest-challenge/

32. Bittner, Jonathan (January 15, 2012). [LinkedIn Post]. Retrieved from http://www.linkedin.com/groupItem?view=&gid=1785140&type=member&item=88674347

33. We recognized that the process of businesses matching what they needed with the communities that have the characteristics desired was broken and that most businesses were without the abilitiy to do data-driven site selection. In 2008, we launched ZoomProspector.com to empower businesses to search nationally for locations to start up, expand, or relocate.

34. Alissa Sklar was not involved with the DBED project, but she was impressed enough with it that she wanted to highlight its success in this case study.

35. Mashable (December 16, 2010). 5 Ways Cities Are Using Social Media to Reverse Economic Downturn [Blog entry]. Retrieved from http://mashable.com/2010/12/16/cities-social-media-recession/

Acknowledgements

Books, like economic development, are team efforts. We are very thankful to all of the people who helped make this book possible. Specifically, we are indebted to all of the economic developers and site selectors who took time to provide information about their work through the national surveys we conducted.

At GIS Planning, we thank Pablo Monzon for his support of this book, as it again took significant staff time away from their day-to-day activities. We appreciate your support and belief that this would not only make our team smarter, but also the entire profession. Additional thanks go to Pau Rodriguez for his design of the book cover and Robyn Cathey for helping in the coordination of the book.

Our deep thanks go to the family of GIS Planning clients who have shown us the very best in online economic development marketing in our profession through their passion and vision. They are an unstoppable movement of innovators of Internet technology that see value and opportunity with clarity.

Acknowledgements from Anatalio Ubalde

Thank you to all of the economic developers I have met who have shared your stories and friendship with me as I have traveled to give talks about economic development and whom I've connected with through my work at GIS Planning, ZoomProspector.com, and Size-Up. You all inspire me to keep innovating and bringing information like this book to our profession.

Thank you to my co-author, Eric Simundza, who tirelessly collected and analyzed data for this book. You are an amazing colleague and friend. It is my honor to have co-authored a second book with you.

Special thanks are given to my wife, Agnes Briones Ubalde, who supports my relentless commitment to economic development service. Lastly, thank you to my three children. It is for you and other children that we are engaged in building a better future through economic development.

Acknowledgements from Eric Simundza

I'd like to thank my co-author Anatalio for his commitment to educating communities; it's an infectious energy that has helped fuel me in this effort. I would also like to thank all of the authors who provided incredible insights in their case studies. Lastly, I'd like to thank my father, Gary Simundza, for passing on his editor's eye and his knack for numbers, and for taking the time to review the work in this book just in case I had not previously absorbed all of his wisdom.

About the Authors

Anatalio Ubalde, MCP, FM

Anatalio Ubalde is an economic developer, entrepreneur, and patent-holder. He is CEO of GIS Planning Inc., an economic development internet company; ZoomProspector.com, an online site selection and business intelligence service; and SizeUp, a small business intelligence service and TechCrunch Disrupt 2011 Finalist. Mr. Ubalde works with organizations throughout the nation to foster enhanced economic development strategies using Internet technology. His company's economic development technology currently serves over 13,000 cities including the majority of the 100 largest cities in the United States. GIS Planning's ZoomProspector Enterprise web-based GIS product is the industry standard for site selection websites in economic development. In the past 5 years in a row, GIS Planning has made the *Inc.* 5000 list of fastest growing private companies in the United States.

His work in geographic information systems, economic development, and the Internet is featured in *The Wall Street Journal, Bloomberg BusinessWeek, Forbes, Fortune, Inc.*, and *The New York Times*. In 2009, he was named a Fellow Member of the International Economic Development Council (IEDC) for achieving exceptional stature in the field of economic development. He is also a Board Member of IEDC.

In 2012, the US Small Business Administration (SBA) made SizeUp a strategic service to small businesses on the SBA website. In this same year, top executives from Google, Facebook, and Salesforce.com selected SizeUp and ZoomProspector.com services as the 1st and 2nd place award winners for online tools to create jobs and grow the US economy, recognizing them through the US Department of Commerce.

Mr. Ubalde is co-author of the book *Economic Development Marketing: Present & Future* (2008) with Eric Simundza, co-author of *Economic Development Online* (2011) with Andrew Krueger, and author of articles in *Economic Development America*, *Economic Development Commentary*, and the *Canadian Economic Development and Technology Journal*. He is a highly sought-after speaker on the subject of Internet and GIS strategies for effective economic development, and has made presentations on these subjects throughout North America, Asia, and Europe.

Before GIS Planning, he worked in local economic development with a focus on downtown revitalization, waterfront redevelopment, business attraction/expansion, business retention, and site selection assistance. He has a Masters degree in City Planning from U.C. Berkeley.

Mr. Ubalde is a twenty-four-time United States Master's Diving National Champion, an All-American, and in 2010 won two silver medals at the World Masters Championships in Gothenburg, Sweden in springboard and platform diving. He is married to Agnes Briones Ubalde and is the father of Anatalio C. Ubalde, IV, Luisa B. Ubalde, and Mario N. Ubalde.

Eric Simundza, MCP

Eric Simundza is a Product Manager at GIS Planning. He led the development of SizeUp, which he manages in addition to ZoomProspector.com.

Mr. Simundza has over a decade of experience in economic development and workforce development. He has consulted with business improvement districts and provided direct technical assistance services to small businesses. At Seedco, he managed multi-million dollar government employment services contracts for a network of ten CBOs in New York City, and also oversaw the launch of a Job Access Reverse Commute (JARC) shuttle service program for low-income workers in Upper Manhattan and the Bronx.

Mr. Simundza has a Master's degree in City Planning from U.C. Berkeley, and has been invited to speak at economic development organizations and conferences across the country. He lives in Oakland, California.